INVESTIGATIONS
SPACE

IAN GRAHAM

CONSULTANT—DR GERAINT H. JONES

LORENZ BOOKS

First published in 1999 by Lorenz Books

© Anness Publishing Limited 1999

Published in the United States by
Lorenz Books, Anness Publishing Inc.,
27 West 20th Street, New York, NY 10011;
(800) 354-9657

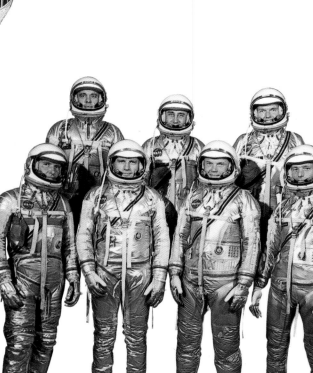

ISBN 1 85967 914 5

Publisher: Joanna Lorenz
Managing Editor, Children's Books: Sue Grabham
Senior Editor: Neil Kelly
Photographer: John Freeman
Stylist: Melanie Williams
Designer: Caroline Grimshaw
Picture Researcher: Kay Rowley
Illustrator: Peter Bull Art Studio
Production Controller: Ann Childers
Editorial Reader: Hayley Kerr

Printed and bound in Singapore

10 9 8 7 6 5 4 3 2 1

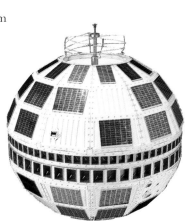

The publishers would like to thank the following children,
and their parents, for modeling in this book—Mohammed Afsar,
Harriet Bartholomew, James Capuyan, Joanne Fleck, Mary Fleck,
Otis Harrington, Stella-Rae James, Tommy Swaine-Jameson, Charlie Ray,
Jackie Ritah.

PICTURE CREDITS
b=bottom, t=top, c=center, l=left, r=right
SPL=Science Photo Library
Anglo-Australian Telescope Board/Image Select page 8tr; Chris Beetles, London, UK/Bridgeman Art Library page 4cr; Daily
Telegraph Colour Library page 44cr; ©1982 Don Dixon/TRH Pictures/NASM/NASA page 9bl; ESA/David Ducros page 62cl;
ESO Information and Photographic Service page 24bl; Genesis Space Photo Library pages 33cr, 33tl, 35tl, 37tl, 40cl, 41b, 56cl, 57cl;
NASA pages 2t, 2br, 3br, 5br, 21tl, 21br, 24br, 34br, 37br, 63tl, 63tr, 63bl, 63br; NASA/Genesis Space Photo Library pages 43tl, 44tl;
NASA/Science and Society Photo Library pages 40cr, 48b; NASA/Space Charts pages 1, 36tr, 36br, 42cl, 45tl, 57br; NASA/SPL
pages 4br, 8br, 19br, 32cl, 32bl, 35br, 40tr, 41tr, 42br, 43tr, 44br, 45bl, 46tl, 47c, 52tl; Novosti Photo Library pages 28cl, 28bl; Planet
Earth Pictures pages 22tl, 25tl, 35bl, 37tr, 37cl, 49tl, 52bl, 53tc, 53cl, 53bl; Science Museum/Science and Society Picture Library
pages 2cl, 34tl, 36cl, 42bl, 53tr, 56tr, 61cr; Space Charts pages 28br, 32t, 42cl; SPL page 26tr; Sally Bensusen (1988)/SPL page 9cr;
Tony Craddock/SPL page 57tr; David Ducros/SPL pages 29cr, 53cr; John Frassanito, NASA/SPL page 49br; Geospace/SPL page 5tl;
Goddard Flight Control Center, Ken M. Johns/SPL page 56bl; David A. Hardy/SPL page 54tr; Tony and Daphne Hallas/SPL page
20tr; Ton Kinsbergen/SPL page 15cr; Marshall Space Flight Center/NASA/SPL page 60cr; Max-Planck-Institut für
Radioastronomie/SPL pages 6br, 25tr; Mehau Kulyk/SPL page 49bl; Naval Research Laboratory/SPL page 7br; Novosti Photo
Library/SPL pages 32br, 34cl, 49l; David Parker/SPL page 25bl; Pekka Parviainen/SPL pages 15cr, 21tl; Rev. Ronald Royer/SPL
pages 15br, 23cr; Rosenfeld Images Ltd/SPL page 61cr; Royal Greenwich Observatory/SPL page 24tl, 24cr; John Sanford/SPL
page 4tl; Joe Tucciarone/SPL page 6cr; Dr Rudolph Schild/SPL page 7bl; US Department of Energy/SPL page 62bl; D. Van
Ravenswaay/SPL page 21tr; TRH Pictures/NASM/NASA page 13tr; TRH Pictures/NASA pages 18tr, 18cl, 33tl, 41tl; NASA/Image
Select page 52br; Ann Ronan/Image Select page 28tl; Space Frontiers page 33bl; TRH Pictures page 45tr; TRH Pictures/Deutsche
Aerospace page 57tl; TRH Pictures/Lockheed-Martin pages 60tl, 64bl; TRH Pictures/M. Roberts page 45br; The Ronald Grant
Archive page 50tl; University of Wisconsin Centre for Space Automation and Robotics/SPL page 62br

SPACE

CONTENTS

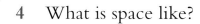

WHAT IS SPACE LIKE?

The night sky

As the sun sinks below the horizon each night and its light fades, the stars begin to appear. They cannot be seen during the day as the sun's light blocks them out. As your eyes become used to the darkness at night, more and more stars can be seen.

LOOK up at the sky on a clear night and you will see the vastness of space, peppered with countless twinkling stars and planets. It looks as though it has been there forever, but once, a very long time ago, there was nothing. The universe did not exist. Most scientists believe that space and everything in it began about 15,000 million years ago with an enormous explosion called the Big Bang. Everything that exists came from the boiling soup of energy that poured out from the Big Bang. Most of the universe is empty, however. Matter is collected together in clumps to form stars and planets, and also in clouds where new stars are forming all the time. There is almost no matter at all in the empty tracts of space that lie between these clumps and clouds. There is no air in space and it is colder than the coldest place on Earth, unless you are near a star.

Galileo Galilei

The Italian scientist Galileo Galilei (1564–1642) was the first person to study the universe with a telescope. He saw mountains on the Earth's Moon and discovered moons orbiting the giant planet Jupiter. He also observed Saturn's rings, although he was unsure what they actually were. Galileo's many discoveries about the stars and planets made him famous all over Europe.

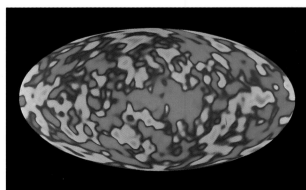

Telescope

Armillary sphere (represents the celestial sphere)

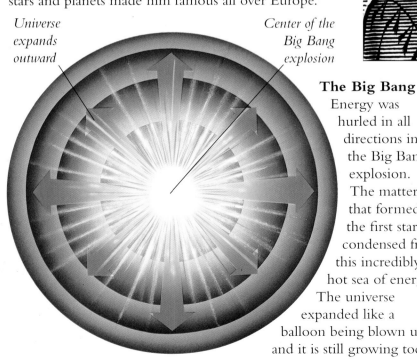

Universe expands outward

Center of the Big Bang explosion

The Big Bang
Energy was hurled in all directions in the Big Bang explosion. The matter that formed the first stars condensed from this incredibly hot sea of energy. The universe expanded like a balloon being blown up, and it is still growing today.

Echoes of the Big Bang
In 1992, a space probe called COBE (COsmic Background Explorer) produced this sky-map. The pink, red and pale blue areas show variations in temperature left over from the Big Bang.

A jewel in space

The colorful Earth stands out like a rare jewel against the blackness of space. The planet's blue oceans, green-carpeted land masses and swirling white clouds all combine to give it a unique appearance. The planet's abundant water and air also make the Earth the only known planet in the solar system capable of supporting life.

Layers of the atmosphere

The Earth is surrounded by a blanket of air called the atmosphere. It is divided into five layers. The lowest layer, troposphere, is where the weather changes occur. It reaches a height of up to 6 miles above the Earth. The stratosphere then reaches up to 25 miles and the mesosphere extends to a height of 40 miles. Above this are the thermosphere and exosphere layers. The air is so thin at this altitude that it fades away through these upper layers into space.

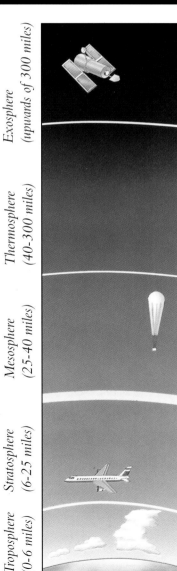

Exosphere (upwards of 300 miles)

Thermosphere (40-300 miles)

Mesosphere (25-40 miles)

Stratosphere (6-25 miles)

Troposphere (0-6 miles)

A human satellite

Space shuttle astronaut Bruce McCandless hangs in space wearing his own one-man spacecraft, the Manned Maneuvering Unit (MMU). He orbits the Earth just like the moon, a space shuttle or a satellite. The astronaut controls and steers the MMU in space by using gas jets operated by hand controls.

GALAXIES

STARS are not spread evenly through space. They are clustered together in vast rotating groups called galaxies. One galaxy may contain thousands of millions of stars. Galaxies are so big that they are measured not in miles, but in light-years. A light-year is the distance light travels in a year, which is about 6 trillion miles. Galaxies are different shapes. Many are giant flat spirals, some are ball-shaped, while others seem to have no particular shape. We live in a spiral galaxy called the Milky Way. Many galaxies can be seen through telescopes. They look like fuzzy patches of light compared to the pinpoints of light that are the stars. The French astronomer Charles Messier (1730-1817) gave numbers to many galaxies. The Andromeda galaxy, for example, is also known by the Messier number M31.

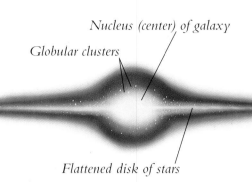

Nucleus (center) of galaxy

Globular clusters

Flattened disk of stars

The Milky Way
Viewed from the side, the Milky Way looks like a thin, flat disk with a bulge in the middle. The Milky Way is 3,000 light years thick, 100,000 light years across, and contains about 100 billion stars.

Above the Milky Way
If you could look down on the Milky Way from above, you would see a beautiful spiral galaxy with glowing arms curling out into space. The sun is a very ordinary star located between two major arms of the Milky Way. It is located about 30,000 light years away from the center of the galaxy.

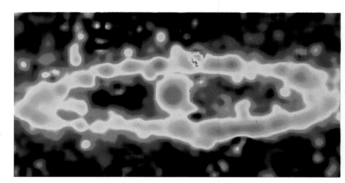

Make a spiral galaxy
Half-fill a 1-quart jar with water. Use a paper punch to cut out about 20 paper circles. Carefully sprinkle the paper circles on the water, and then stir the water gently. See how the paper circles form a flattened rotating spiral, just like a spiral galaxy.

Radio astronomy
This is a radio picture of the Andromeda galaxy. Galaxies give out several forms of energy. Pictures can be made that show the types of energy. The colors in this image show the varying amounts of radio waves coming from different parts of Andromeda.

Elliptical galaxies

There are four main types of galaxies—elliptical, spiral, barred spiral and irregular. Elliptical galaxies are the most common, and may be ball-shaped or egg-shaped.

Spiral galaxies

A typical spiral galaxy is shaped like a flattened disk with a bulge in the middle, called the nucleus. The nucleus is surrounded by the curling spiral arms.

Barred spiral galaxies

A barred spiral is a type of spiral galaxy with an elongated, bar-shaped nucleus. Its spiral arms extend outwards from the ends of the bar.

Irregular galaxies

An irregular galaxy is unlike other galaxies as it has no particular shape. The Large Magellanic Cloud, one of the closest galaxies to Earth, is an irregular galaxy.

X-ray view of a galaxy

The High Energy Astronomy Observatory satellite HEAO-1 took this X-ray picture of the Milky Way in 1977. X rays are the same sort of energy waves that doctors use when they need to look inside your body. False colors were added to the picture to show the many different sources of X rays in the galaxy. The energy waves are given out by areas in space where large quantities of very hot gas are present. The temperature of the gas found in these areas can be as high as 1½ million°F.

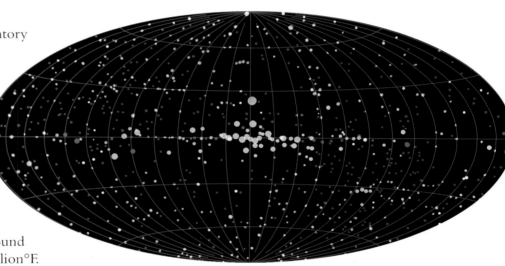

Center of galaxy

M87 is an elliptical galaxy

Jet of plasma 5,000 light years long

Galactic giant

A jet of particles shoots out from the center of this false-color image of the M87 galaxy. M87 is so big that light takes 40,000 years to cross it. The galaxy is surrounded by hundreds of clumps of stars called globular clusters, each of which contains about a million stars.

FACT BOX

• The biggest known galaxy is 5,600,000 light years across. It is located about 1,000 million light years away in the constellation Virgo.

• The most distant galaxies found so far are more than 13,000 million light years away from Earth.

• The Milky Way belongs to a collection of about 30 galaxies called the Local Group. These galaxies move through space together.

WHAT IS A STAR?

A STAR is a giant ball of gas. Most of it is hydrogen, the lightest gas of all. At the center, particles of matter smash into each other with such incredible force that they fuse together, releasing a burst of energy. This is called nuclear fusion. Most stars can release energy steadily for thousands of millions of years. Stars are formed in giant clouds of dust and gas called nebulae. Clumps of matter inside a nebula attract more and more matter towards them. Each clump grows bigger and bigger until nuclear fusion starts. The nuclear reactions create heat and light, and the star begins to shine. It burns brightly for thousands of millions of years, until no more hydrogen is left. Small stars then shrink to become white dwarfs. Large stars change into objects called neutron stars. Black holes are created when massive stars collapse.

Stellar birthplace
The Orion Nebula is the birthplace for hundreds of stars. It is a vast cloud of dust and gas in which new stars are forming. When viewed through a telescope, the cloud appears to glow brightly. It is illuminated by the many stars that have already formed inside it.

How a star forms

 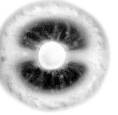    

1. Clumps of dust and gas inside a nebula condense to form spinning objects called protostars.

2. Each protostar becomes very tightly packed and attracts more dust and gas toward it by gravity.

3. Nuclear fusion begins, pouring out energy and blowing away surrounding gas and dust.

4. The remaining dust and gas form a flattened disk of matter orbiting around the star.

5. The disk of debris may eventually form planets and moons, as it did around our own star, the sun.

6. The star begins to shine as hydrogen atoms in its core join to form helium.

Supernova remnant
This false-color photograph shows the light energy given off by the Crab Nebula. A nebula is a cloud of gas and dust thrown out into space when a massive star explodes. The explosion is known as a supernova. Chinese astronomers recorded the explosion that formed the Crab Nebula when it took place in 1054. The supernova was bright enough to be seen during the day. The remains of the star can be seen at the center of the false-color picture. The colors run from red for the brightest regions of the nebula and fade to yellow, green, blue and gray.

Life cycle of an average-sized star

Most stars change hydrogen into helium for thousands of millions of years. This period is called the main sequence. When an average-sized star like the sun runs out of hydrogen, it does not explode in a supernova like a massive star. Instead, it begins converting helium into carbon and expands into a red giant. When the helium runs out, the star ejects its outer layers. It then shrinks, becoming a white dwarf. Finally, the white dwarf cools to become a black dwarf.

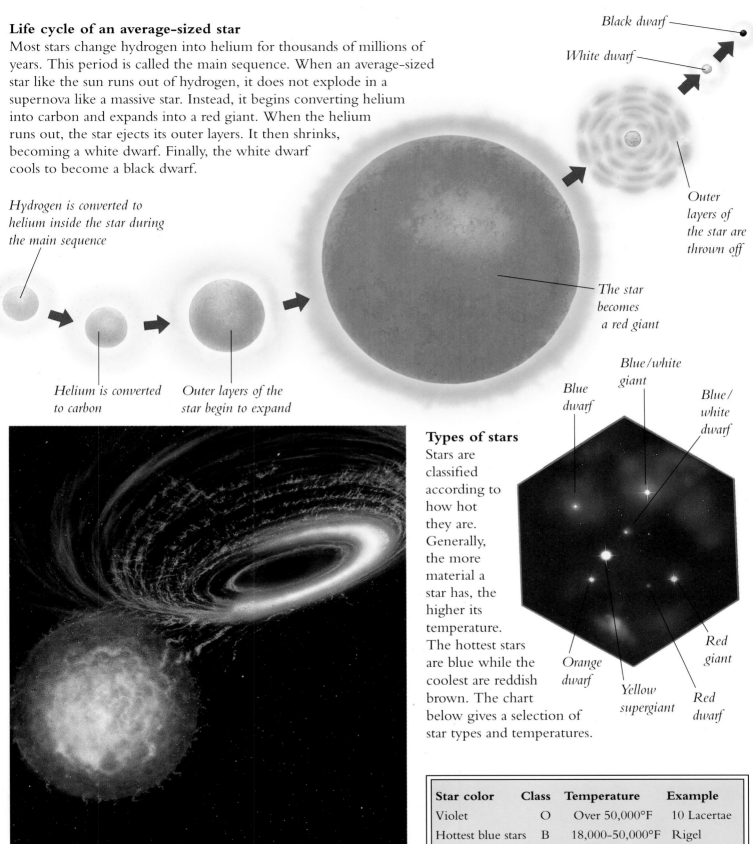

Hydrogen is converted to helium inside the star during the main sequence

Helium is converted to carbon

Outer layers of the star begin to expand

The star becomes a red giant

Outer layers of the star are thrown off

Black dwarf

White dwarf

Blue dwarf

Blue/white giant

Blue/white dwarf

Orange dwarf

Yellow supergiant

Red dwarf

Red giant

Types of stars

Stars are classified according to how hot they are. Generally, the more material a star has, the higher its temperature. The hottest stars are blue while the coolest are reddish brown. The chart below gives a selection of star types and temperatures.

Holes in space

Stellar matter spirals into a black hole. When a massive star explodes, the dense, collapsed core that is left generates a strong gravitational field. A black hole is formed when the field is so strong that it bends space into an invisible one-way funnel. Not even light can escape from the black hole's pull of gravity.

Star color	Class	Temperature	Example
Violet	O	Over 50,000°F	10 Lacertae
Hottest blue stars	B	18,000–50,000°F	Rigel
Blue star	A	13,500–18,000°F	Sirius
Blue/white	F	10,800–13,500°F	Canopus
White/yellow	G	9,000–10,800°F	The sun
Orange/red	K	6,300–9,000°F	Arcturus
Red	M	Less than 6,300°F	Betelgeuse

PULSARS AND BLACK HOLES

Pulsars and black holes are two of the strangest types of objects in the universe. Pulsars are spinning neutron stars that send out regular pulses of radio energy. They are formed from the collapsed cores of exploded stars that were originally six to eight times the size of the sun. A pulsar sends out a narrow beam of radio waves as it sweeps around the sky. As the pulsar is rotating, the radio beam appears to flash on and off, like the light from a lighthouse. Black holes are produced when even bigger stars collapse. The core that is left cools, as nuclear reactions are no longer taking place to produce heat. This reduces the pressure pushing outward from within the star. Gravity pulls the star's material towards its center. If the force of gravity is strong enough, the star continues to shrink until it is no longer visible. It has become a black hole. Follow these projects to make a flashing pulsar and to demonstrate how a black hole forms.

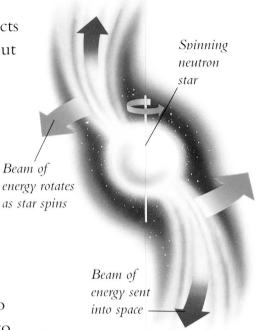

Spinning neutron star

Beam of energy rotates as star spins

Beam of energy sent into space

Neutron stars

As the core of an exploded massive star collapses, it begins to spin rapidly. The core is also called a neutron star, as it is made from tightly packed neutron particles. Pulsars are spinning neutron stars that send out energy pulses many times per second. The types of energy sent out include light, X rays and radio waves.

MAKE A PULSAR

You will need: ruler, string, scissors, door frame, tape, flashlight.

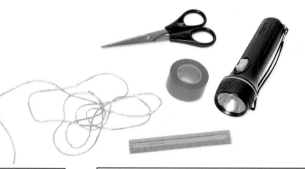

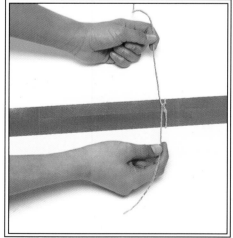

1 Measure out 24 inches of string using a ruler. Cut the string with scissors. Tie or tape one end of the string to a door frame. Be careful not to damage the frame's surface.

2 Wrap the other end of the string around the center of the flashlight. Tie it in a knot. Tape the string to the flashlight to secure it. Make sure that the flashlight can spin around freely.

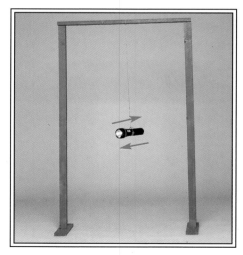

3 With the curtains closed and the lights off, spin the flashlight around. As the light sweeps around the room, it appears to blink on and off like a pulsar's radio beams.

1 Place one of the jars on top of a work surface. Attach a round balloon to a balloon pump. Dangle the balloon so that half of it is inside the jar and half of it is outside.

2 Blow up the balloon. Ask a friend to tie a piece of string around the balloon's neck to keep the air in. Now repeat steps 1 and 2 with the second balloon and jar.

3 Using a permanent marker, carefully mark a line on each balloon along the top of each jar. Make sure you do not press too hard, as this may pop the balloons.

FORMING A BLACK HOLE

You will need:
2 large-mouthed glass jars,
2 small round balloons,
balloon pump, string,
permanent marker.

One-way trip
A black hole bends space into a deep funnel. Nearby matter is sucked in, disappearing altogether from the universe.

Entrance to black hole

Funnel of black hole

4 Put one jar, with the balloon half inside and half outside, in a freezer. After 30 minutes remove the jar and balloon. The balloon has sunk into the jar, as shown.

5 Compare the chilled balloon with the balloon that has remained at room temperature. The chilled balloon has sunk into its jar, but the other balloon has not. As the air particles inside the chilled balloon grew colder, they packed closer together, reducing the pressure inside the balloon. This caused the stretchy rubber to shrink, like a star's core collapsing under its own gravity to form a black hole.

CONSTELLATIONS

DURING the night, stars seem to rise and set as the Earth rotates. As the months go by, new stars come into view as the Earth moves in its orbit around the sun. People have looked at the night sky and spotted patterns in the stars for thousands of years. Finding patterns made it easier to follow the movements of the stars across the sky. In ancient times few people had written calendars. Instead they followed the passing of time by looking at the movements of stars. It was important to know when certain stars appeared in the sky, because they marked the times when crops should be planted or harvested, or when migrating animals would return and could be killed for food. In the ancient world, people named groups of stars after the heroes and creatures of their legends. The ancient Greeks divided the stars into 48 groups called constellations, 12 of which form the signs of the Zodiac. Another 40 constellations have since been added, making a total of 88.

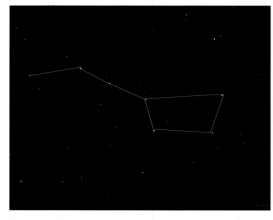

Star patterns
The Big Dipper (also called the Plough) is a familiar sight in the sky in the Northern Hemisphere. It is formed from seven stars in Ursa Major (Great Bear). Ursa Major is one of the oldest constellations and is easy to find in the sky.

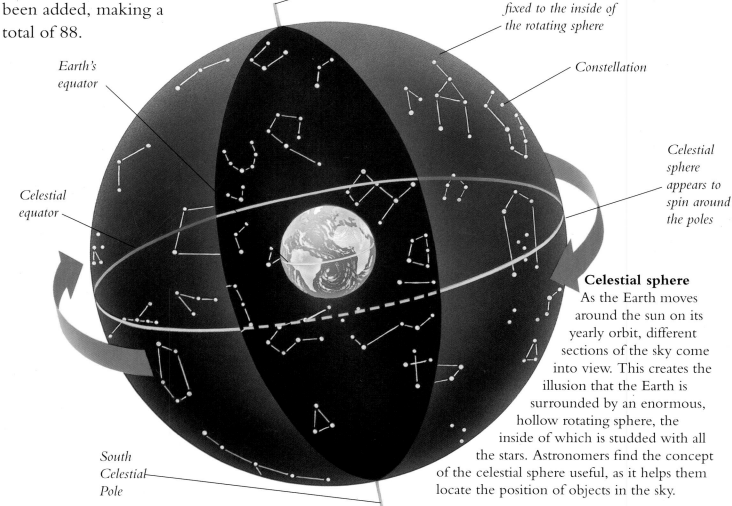

North Celestial Pole

Earth's equator

Stars appear to be fixed to the inside of the rotating sphere

Constellation

Celestial equator

Celestial sphere appears to spin around the poles

South Celestial Pole

Celestial sphere
As the Earth moves around the sun on its yearly orbit, different sections of the sky come into view. This creates the illusion that the Earth is surrounded by an enormous, hollow rotating sphere, the inside of which is studded with all the stars. Astronomers find the concept of the celestial sphere useful, as it helps them locate the position of objects in the sky.

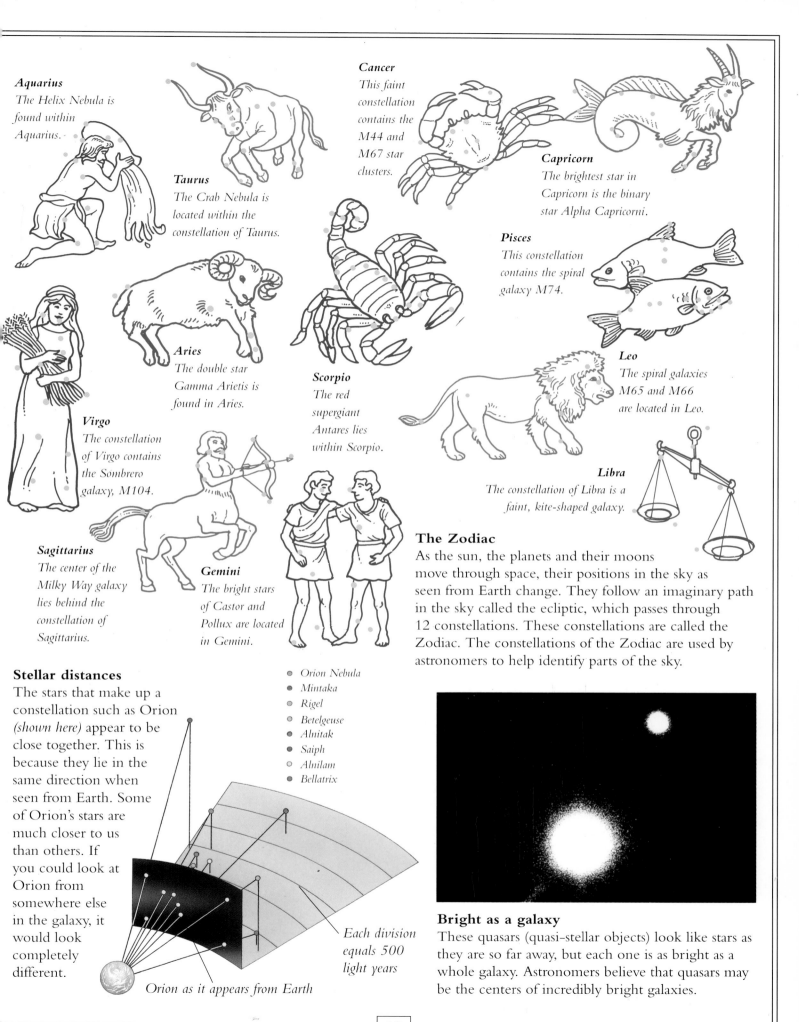

Aquarius
The Helix Nebula is found within Aquarius.

Taurus
The Crab Nebula is located within the constellation of Taurus.

Cancer
This faint constellation contains the M44 and M67 star clusters.

Capricorn
The brightest star in Capricorn is the binary star Alpha Capricorni.

Pisces
This constellation contains the spiral galaxy M74.

Aries
The double star Gamma Arietis is found in Aries.

Scorpio
The red supergiant Antares lies within Scorpio.

Leo
The spiral galaxies M65 and M66 are located in Leo.

Virgo
The constellation of Virgo contains the Sombrero galaxy, M104.

Libra
The constellation of Libra is a faint, kite-shaped galaxy.

Sagittarius
The center of the Milky Way galaxy lies behind the constellation of Sagittarius.

Gemini
The bright stars of Castor and Pollux are located in Gemini.

The Zodiac

As the sun, the planets and their moons move through space, their positions in the sky as seen from Earth change. They follow an imaginary path in the sky called the ecliptic, which passes through 12 constellations. These constellations are called the Zodiac. The constellations of the Zodiac are used by astronomers to help identify parts of the sky.

Stellar distances

The stars that make up a constellation such as Orion *(shown here)* appear to be close together. This is because they lie in the same direction when seen from Earth. Some of Orion's stars are much closer to us than others. If you could look at Orion from somewhere else in the galaxy, it would look completely different.

- Orion Nebula
- Mintaka
- Rigel
- Betelgeuse
- Alnitak
- Saiph
- Alnilam
- Bellatrix

Each division equals 500 light years

Orion as it appears from Earth

Bright as a galaxy

These quasars (quasi-stellar objects) look like stars as they are so far away, but each one is as bright as a whole galaxy. Astronomers believe that quasars may be the centers of incredibly bright galaxies.

THE SUN, OUR STAR

THE sun is an ordinary star, but it is very special to us because it is by far the closest star to the Earth. At about 93,300,000 miles away, it is also the only star we can see by eye that is larger than a pinpoint. At that distance, it provides just the right amount of heat and light to support life here on Earth. The sun is a massive ball of gas, composed mostly of hydrogen and helium. It is a giant nuclear reactor, converting about four million tons of hydrogen into helium, heat and light every second. Just over half of the energy given out by the sun is visible light and most of the rest is heat. Its temperature reaches an incredible 27,000,000°F at the center, falling to about 9,900°F at its gassy surface. The sun is a truly enormous object. Its gravity dominates the solar system as it is so massive in comparison to the planets. The sun is more than 332,000 times heavier than the Earth. It measures a massive 864,000 miles in linear diameter, compared to less than 7,928 miles for the Earth. Our star is roughly halfway through its life-span of about 10,000 million years.

Convection zone

Radiative zone

Solar prominence

Supergranule (convection cell)

Sunspot

Solar wind

Trapped solar wind particles glow as the aurorae when they hit the atmosphere

Magnetotail

The magnetosphere acts as a buffer between the Earth's upper atmosphere and the solar wind

The Earth

The Van Allen radiation belts are located above the Earth's equator

Magnetosphere

The Earth is a giant magnet, surrounded by a field of magnetic forces in a region called the magnetosphere. This field stretches far out into space. The sun sends out streams of particles called solar wind, which squeeze the Earth's magnetosphere on the side nearest the sun. This gives the magnetosphere an elongated teardrop shape. The long magnetotail on the side of the Earth facing away from the sun can stretch as far as the moon's orbit.

Core
(27,000,000°F)

Photosphere
(9,900°F)

Aurora borealis
Solar wind particles raining down on the Earth's poles produce spectacular colored lights in the sky. These are called aurorae. An aurora at the North Pole *(shown left)* is called an aurora borealis. An aurora appearing at the South Pole is called an aurora australis.

Solar probe
In 1995, the SOHO space probe (SOlar and Heliospheric Observatory) was launched to study the sun. It orbits the sun 930,000 miles from Earth, at a point where the sun's pull of gravity exactly balances the pull of the Earth. Space probes like SOHO warn scientists when Earth's magnetosphere might be affected by solar storms.

Inside the sun
The stormy surface of the sun boils furiously as energy pours out from its core. Curling tongues of fiery gas bigger than the Earth are often flung out into space. These are called solar prominences. Dark spots called sunspots often appear on the sun's surface. They are caused by magnetic disturbances within the star. Sunspots are areas of cooler gas that appear to be black in contrast to their hotter, brighter surroundings.

FACT BOX

• The sun creates energy at the same rate as a trillion hydrogen bombs exploding each second!

• The number of sunspots on the sun's surface reaches a peak every 11 years.

• The sun is 30,000 light years from the center of the Milky Way galaxy.

• The sun takes roughly 25 days to make one rotation at the equator. At the poles it rotates more slowly, taking about 35 days to make one rotation.

Solar eclipse
When the moon's orbit causes it to pass directly between the Earth and the sun, a total solar eclipse occurs. With the sun's blinding light blocked out by the moon, the star's gassy outer atmosphere, called the corona, can be clearly seen.

ORBITS AND DISTANCES

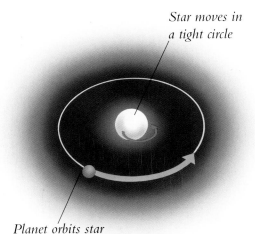

Star moves in a tight circle

Planet orbits star

Wobbling star
A planet's gravity pulls the star it orbits around in a tight circle, making the star appear to wobble. Planets orbiting distant stars are too small to be seen, but by looking for telltale wobble, astronomers have detected stars that may have planets...

S OLAR systems and galaxies are held together by the invisible force of gravity generated by stars, planets and other stellar bodies. Gravity causes moons to orbit (circle) around planets, planets to orbit stars and stars to orbit the center of the galaxy. An orbit is a balancing act. A star's gravity pulls a planet toward it. This is balanced by the planet's natural tendency to travel in a straight line, rather than circling around the star. Try making your own modeling clay planet orbiting a modeling clay star. In your model, the star's gravitational pull is simulated by the downward pull on a piece of string of the clay star. Constellations of stars are not held together by gravity in the same way as solar systems. The stars in a constellation such as Orion appear close together as they lie in the same direction when seen from Earth. By making a model of Orion, you can see that its shape and the distance between its stars would look very different from elsewhere in the galaxy.

MAKE A PLANET ORBITING A STAR

You will need: string, scissors, ballpoint pen barrel, paper clips, modeling clay.

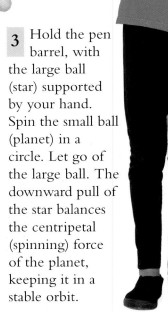

Orbiting planet

Star

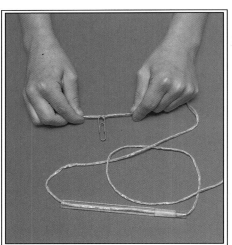

1 Cut a piece of string to about 18 inches in length. Thread the piece of string through the ballpoint pen barrel. Tie a paper clip to each end of the string.

2 Divide the modeling clay into two lumps, one twice the size of the other. Roll each lump of clay into a ball. Push a paper clip into each ball, as shown.

3 Hold the pen barrel, with the large ball (star) supported by your hand. Spin the small ball (planet) in a circle. Let go of the large ball. The downward pull of the star balances the centripetal (spinning) force of the planet, keeping it in a stable orbit.

MAKE A MODEL OF ORION

1 Cut out 2 pieces of cardboard, each measuring 4 inches x 2¼ inches. Then cut out 2 pieces of cardboard measuring 9½ inches x 2¼ inches, and 1 piece of cardboard measuring 4 inches x 9½ inches.

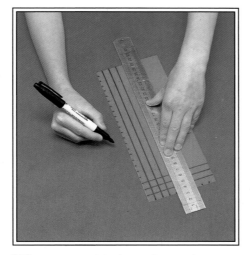

2 Using the black marker and a ruler, draw a grid of ½-inch squares on the 4 x 9½-inch cardboard. The 4-inch edge forms an X axis, and the 9½-inch edge forms a Y axis.

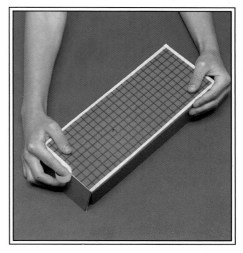

3 Tape the pieces together to form a box. Mark the X axis with an X and number the squares from 1 to 10. Mark the Y axis with a Y and number from 1 to 24.

You will need: cardboard, ruler, scissors, markers (red and black), tape, wooden skewers, modeling clay.

Star	X axis	Y axis	Length
Betelgeuse	1/2 in	2¼ in	6¾ in
Bellatrix	2¾ in	1¾ in	6½ in
Alnitak	1¾ in	7 in	3¾ in
Alnilam	2 in	7 in	4 in
Mintaka	2¼ in	7 in	4 in
Saiph	1 in	8⅓ in	1¼ in
Rigel	3¾ in	4 in	1¾ in

Familiar stars
The three bright stars that form Orion's belt stand out very clearly, making it easy to spot. Orion can be seen from both the northern and southern hemispheres of the Earth.

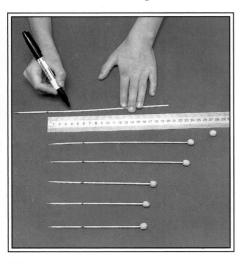

4 Using the red marker, mark 7 wooden skewers 2¼ inches from the point. Cut them to the lengths shown in the table and attach a clay star to each end.

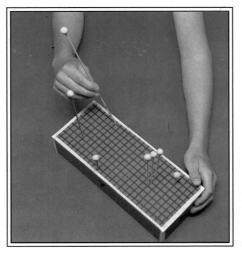

5 Using the X and Y co-ordinates for each star shown in the table, push the skewers through the top of the box. Make sure they are pushed through up to the red marks.

6 To view Orion as it is seen from Earth, position the box as shown above. If you look at the model from the side, the constellation will form a completely different shape.

THE SOLAR SYSTEM

THE solar system is made up of the sun, the planets, their moons and every other object that is influenced by the sun's gravity. It was created about 4,600 million years ago from a cloud of dust and gas. Its formation may have been triggered by an exploding star nearby. Nine planets follow endless orbits around the sun, trapped by its invisible but immensely powerful pull of gravity. The inner planets of Mercury, Venus, Earth and Mars are small rocky worlds, while most of the outer planets of Jupiter, Saturn, Uranus and Neptune are giants made mainly from gas and liquid. Pluto, an icy, rocky planet smaller than the Earth's moon, is usually the most distant planet, but part of its orbit swings inside Neptune's path. For a few years of Pluto's marathon 248 year long orbit, Neptune is the most distant planet. Most of the planets have moons circling them. Only the planets Mercury and Venus have no moons at all.

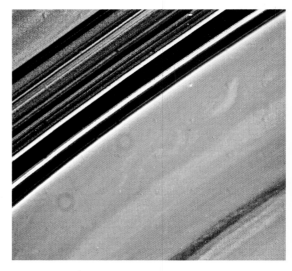

Saturn's rings
The beautiful rings of the planet Saturn are actually made of countless pieces of rock and ice. They form a flat disk around the planet's equator and range in size from tiny particles of dust to lumps the size of a house.

Volcanoes on Mars
Space probes have found volcanoes on several planets in the solar system and at least one moon. This clay model shows Olympus Mons on Mars, the largest known volcano in the Solar System. It is about 310 miles across and reaches a height of 16 miles. Olympus Mons is about three times as high as Earth's tallest mountain, Mount Everest.

Mercury orbits the sun once every 88 days, only 36 million miles away from its searing heat. The tiny planet roasts on one side and freezes on the other.

Venus is a hothouse planet covered by thick clouds. It appears in the sky as a bright star.

Earth is the largest of the rocky inner planets. Most of its surface is covered by water.

Mars is also known as the Red Planet, as it is covered by red dust. Its surface often disappears under fierce dust storms. The planet has polar ice caps made from frozen carbon dioxide that grow and shrink with the changing seasons.

THE SUN

Planets' relative distance from the sun (below)

Merc... Venus Earth Mars

Jupiter

Saturn

Uran...

In the blink of an eye

Scientists believe that the Solar System formed from a cloud of gas and dust in a relatively short time. It probably took about 100 million years from the moment the cloud started to collapse until the sun burst into fiery life. This may seem to be a very long time in human terms, but compared to the age of the universe it is a mere blink of a cosmic eye.

Pluto is a tiny, rocky planet. Its orbit around the sun is tilted at 17°. The orbit of the moon Charon around Pluto is synchronized with the planet's own rotation period of 6.4 days.

Neptune is covered by white and blue clouds made of frozen methane. A Great Dark Spot in its atmosphere appears to be a giant storm like Jupiter's Great Red Spot. One of Neptune's eight moons, Triton, is similar in size to Earth's moon.

The planet Uranus is tipped over on its side. The green-blue planet is a gas giant, like Jupiter. It takes 84 years to orbit the sun. It looks the same all over, as its hazy atmosphere receives little heat from the sun or from inside the planet.

Saturn is surrounded by a system of broad flat rings. About every 14 years the rings are tilted so that they are seen edge-on from Earth.

The gas giant Jupiter is the biggest planet in the solar system. It has a mass two and a half times greater than all the other planets put together. Jupiter rotates very quickly—once every 10 hours. Its four largest moons, discovered by Galileo, can be seen with binoculars. Jupiter has 16 moons in total.

Jovian hurricane

Jupiter's Great Red Spot was discovered in 1664 by the English scientist Robert Hooke. The massive hurricane-like storm is still raging today. It measures 25,000 miles long by 6,800 miles wide. Three planets the size of the Earth could fit along the length of the Spot.

Great Red Spot

Ammonia clouds

Neptune

Pluto

COMETS AND METEORS

CHUNKS of rock, ice and dust left over from the formation of the solar system still orbit the sun today. Some of them are asteroids that range from microscopic grains of dust to pieces of rock almost as large as small planets. It is thought that lumps of ice and rock orbit the sun far beyond the most distant planet. Collisions and the pull of gravity from the outer planets sometimes draw one of them in toward the sun. As it nears the sun, dust and gas are driven off it and swept back into a tail, forming a comet. Sunlight reflects off the dust, and the gas glows. Some comets follow an orbit that brings them back within sight of the Earth at regular intervals. The most famous of these is Halley's Comet. When a meteoroid (a grain of space dust) ploughs into the Earth's atmosphere from space, it is heated so much by friction (rubbing) with the air that it glows and turns to vapor. This forms a shooting star, or meteor. A larger piece of rock that is big enough to reach the ground before it burns up is called a meteorite.

Comet Hale-Bopp
This comet was discovered by astronomers Alan Hale and Thomas Bopp in 1995. The last time the comet's orbit brought it in range of the Earth was 4,000 years ago. Since then, the gravitational pull of the planets has changed its orbit. As a result, it will next pass the Earth in about 2,380 years.

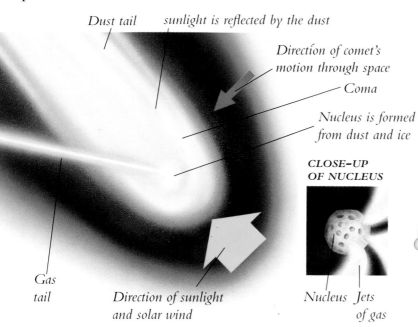

Dust tail — sunlight is reflected by the dust

Direction of comet's motion through space

Coma

Nucleus is formed from dust and ice

CLOSE-UP OF NUCLEUS

Gas tail

Direction of sunlight and solar wind

Nucleus Jets of gas

Inside a comet
The solid part of a comet is called its nucleus. The fuzzy ball that we see is a cloud of gas and dust, called the coma, that surrounds the comet's nucleus. As it nears the sun, the solar wind and sunlight sweeps some of the coma back into a tail.

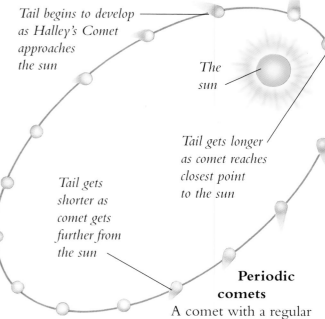

Tail begins to develop as Halley's Comet approaches the sun

The sun

Tail gets longer as comet reaches closest point to the sun

Tail gets shorter as comet gets further from the sun

Periodic comets
A comet with a regular orbit that brings it close to the sun is called a periodic comet. Halley's Comet, for example, orbits the sun every 76 years. When it last returned in 1986, the space probe *Giotto* flew close to it and took pictures of the comet's nucleus.

Types of meteorite

This meteorite is made of rock. There are three main types of meteorite—irons, stony and stony irons. Irons are made of metal. Stony meteorites are rocky. Stony irons are a mix of rock and metal.

Fireworks in the sky

A shower of meteors streak through the sky. Meteor showers take place when the Earth's orbit takes it through debris left behind by passing comets. The dust and rocks burn up in the atmosphere, creating a spectacular fireworks display.

The biggest meteorites create the deepest craters

Smaller meteorites make shallower craters

Making meteor craters

Fill a deep tray or bowl with sand. Drop balls of different sizes and weights into the tray, and see how they make craters. Experiment to see the different types of craters formed when you drop the balls at different angles and speeds.

Impact with the Earth

When a large meteorite hits the ground, it gouges out a crater. Meteor Crater in Arizona is about 3,900 feet across and was created when an iron meteorite weighing 25 tons hit the ground 50,000 years ago. Most craters on Earth are worn away over time by wind and water.

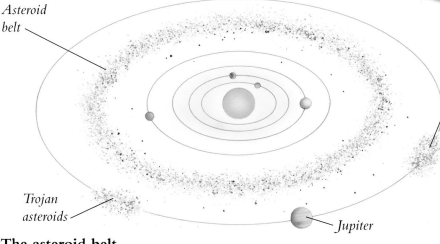

Asteroid belt

Trojan asteroids

Trojan asteroids

Jupiter

Space rock

Asteroid 243 Ida is a typical asteroid. It is a jagged chunk of dust-covered space rock, measuring 32 miles in length. The asteroid's dusty surface is pitted with craters caused by collisions with other asteroids and meteoroids.

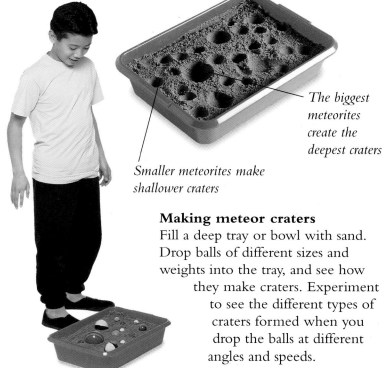

The asteroid belt

Millions of asteroids lie in a broad belt between the orbits of Mars and Jupiter. The largest, Ceres, is about 584 miles across. It was the first to be discovered, in 1801. The orbits of more than 5,000 asteroids are now known. Two more groups of asteroids called the Trojans share the same orbit as Jupiter.

SOLAR HEAT AND WIND

Hothouse planet
This picture shows Venus without its thick cloud layers, revealing the planet's scorched surface. Mercury is the closest planet to the sun, but Venus has a higher surface temperature. This is because its dense cloud layer traps more of the sun's heat, like a greenhouse.

Nearly half of the energy given out by the sun is heat. Infrared (heat) rays produced by the sun travel away from the star into space. Anything that the rays hit absorbs them and becomes warmer. As the rays get further away from the sun, they spread out and their heating power weakens. You can see this effect yourself by carrying out a simple heating experiment with a lamp, a yardstick and two thermometers. The sun also sends out a fast-moving stream of particles called the solar wind. This effect can be observed when a comet approaches the sun. The streams of solar wind particles carry gas from the comet backward to form a tail. As the comet approaches the sun, the tail stretches out behind it. However, as the comet travels away from the sun, it moves tail first. The fast stream of particles sent out by the sun ensure that the tail of the comet is always pointing away from the star. You can demonstrate how the solar wind produces a comet's long gas-tail by performing a simple but effective experiment that uses paint, water and a tray.

HEATING PLANETS

You will need:
yardstick,
2 thermometers,
desk lamp.

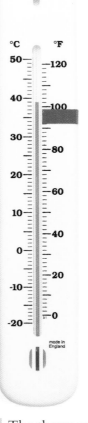

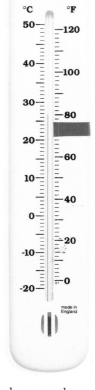

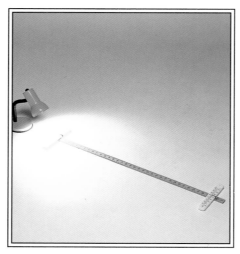

1 Lay the ruler on the ground. Place one thermometer at 4 inches and the other at 40 inches. Place the lamp at the 0-inch end of the ruler.

2 Adjust the lamp so it shines on the thermometer at 4 inches. Turn on the lamp. After 10–15 minutes, compare the two thermometers.

3 The thermometer closer to the lamp is hotter. Similarly, planets closest to the sun are heated more than those that are farther away.

MAKE A COMET

You will need: small tray,
plastic bowl,
paint, paintbrush,
watering can, water.

1 Take the tray and place it on end in the bowl. Make sure that the underside of the tray faces forward so that water can run freely over it.

2 Dip the paintbrush in the paint. Carefully place a thick blob of the paint at the top of the tray, roughly in the middle.

3 Fill the watering can with water. Gently pour the water over the top of the paint blob comet. The paint streams away from the comet, creating a long tail behind the blob nucleus. The water behaves like the solar wind, sweeping gas from the comet back to form a long gas tail.

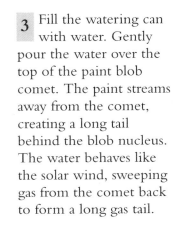

Nucleus of comet

Tail of comet

A tale of two tails
Comet West streaks past the Earth, displaying its spectacular glowing tails. Comets can have one or two tails. This depends on what the comet is made from and how close it approaches the Sun. When Comet West passed by the Earth in 1976, it had a glowing white dust-tail and a blue gas-tail.

ASTRONOMY

THE scientific study of the universe is called astronomy. Astronomers use telescopes to help them study the stars. Optical telescopes use either lenses or mirrors to make distant objects look bigger and brighter. Lens telescopes are also called refractors, while mirror telescopes are called reflectors. Most large astronomical telescopes are reflectors. Telescopes are often built on top of mountains, where the thin, clear air and dark skies give the best views. Stars give out other types of energy as well as light, including radio waves. The Earth's atmosphere stops some types of star energy, such as X rays, from reaching the ground. X-ray telescopes have to be launched into space, so that they can be used outside the atmosphere.

View from a volcano
The William Herschel Telescope (WHT) is located about 7,800 feet above sea level on top of an extinct volcano on La Palma, in the Canary Islands. The high altitude provides an excellent view of the stars.

ESO Telescope
The European Southern Observatory (ESO) New Technology Telescope (NTT) is one of 15 astronomical instruments at La Silla observatory in Chile. Its main mirror is 11¾ feet across. The NTT first began operating in 1989. Its performance was improved with an upgrade in 1997.

Lightweight skeleton frame

Primary mirror

Moving mirror
The WHT's giant 13¾ foot diameter primary mirror is given a final polishing using a special machine. It is one of the most accurately shaped mirrors in the world.

Motors adjust position of telescope

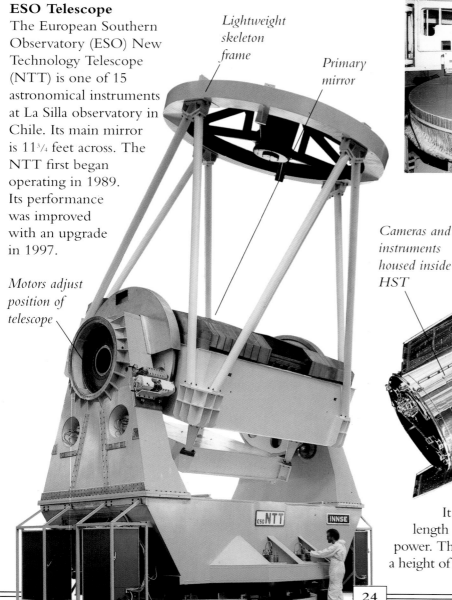

Radio dish antenna

Cameras and instruments housed inside HST

Solar panels provide electricity

Aperture door

Hubble Space Telescope
In 1990, the Space Shuttle launched the Hubble Space Telescope (HST) into orbit around the Earth. It is an optical telescope that measures about 44 feet in length and about 14 feet across. Solar panels provide it with power. The HST weighs nearly 11 tons and orbits the Earth at a height of 370 miles. It sends its images back to Earth by radio.

Linking telescopes

The Very Large Array (VLA) points skywards. The VLA is a group of 27 movable radio telescopes in New Mexico. Each dish measures 82 feet across. The dishes are linked together so that they behave like parts of one huge, 19-mile wide dish.

Arecibo radio telescope

The world's biggest radio telescope is built in a natural hollow in the ground near the city of Arecibo in Puerto Rico. The Arecibo dish is 1,000 feet across and is fixed in position. To scan the sky, motors steer the receiver suspended above the dish.

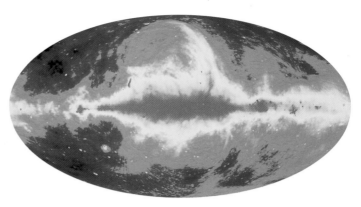

Radio pictures

This image shows radio energy from the Milky Way. Radio telescopes measure the strength of radio energy coming from different points in the sky. The energy strength at each point can be turned into brightness. False colors are added to make a color picture.

Anybody out there?

In 1974, this message was transmitted into the depths of space using the Arecibo radio telescope. It contains a simple representation of a human being, and was directed at a star cluster in the constellation of Hercules. It also shows the location of the solar system within the Milky Way galaxy. If intelligent alien creatures ever receive and process the transmission, they should be able to understand where the message came from. They should also be able to figure out what sort of beings sent it.

FACT BOX

• The world's largest maneuverable radio telescope is the 328-foot wide dish in Effelsberg, Germany. It can be steered to point at any part of the sky.

• After the Hubble Space Telescope was launched in 1990, a fault was discovered in its primary mirror that caused its pictures to be blurred. In 1993, space shuttle astronauts visited the HST and corrected the fault.

LOOKING INTO SPACE

Greenwich Observatory
The Royal Observatory in Greenwich, England was founded by King Charles II in 1675. The King paid for the building, but the astronomer had to buy his own telescopes!

OPTICAL telescopes work by bending light rays, making objects appear closer and larger than is actually the case. They bend light in two different ways. Refracting telescopes use lenses. Light rays from distant objects change direction as they enter the lens and again as they leave it. There are difficulties involved in making very big lenses, so most of the telescopes used in astronomy are of the reflecting type. These telescopes use mirrors instead of lenses. A reflecting telescope's main mirror is curved, so that light rays hitting it bounce off at an angle. Our brains work out how big an object is by analyzing the angle of the light rays from it as the rays enter our eyes. Telescopes use lenses or mirrors to change this angle, tricking our brain into thinking that the light has come from a much bigger object. You can see how both refracting telescopes and reflecting telescopes work by carrying out these simple experiments using lenses and mirrors.

MAKE A SINGLE-MIRROR REFLECTING TELESCOPE

You will need: desk lamp, thick purple paper, marker, scissors, tape, small mirror, magnifying glass, modeling clay.

Starlight — *Eyepiece lens* — *Primary mirror reflects an upside-down image*
Secondary mirror corrects image

Reflecting telescope
Light reflects off the primary mirror. The light rays bounce off a small secondary mirror and are focused and magnified by an eyepiece.

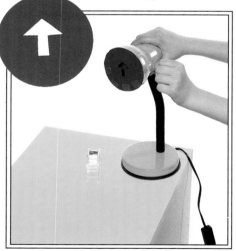

1 Trace a circle around the head of the lamp on a sheet of purple paper. Cut it out. Then cut out a central arrow *(shown above)*. Stick the circle onto the front of the lamp.

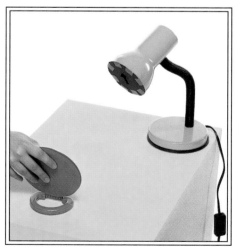

2 Set up the desk lamp and mirror so that the mirror reflects the light from the lamp onto a nearby wall. Use modeling clay to help support the mirror, if necessary.

3 Set up the magnifying glass so that light reflecting from the mirror passes through it. The lens magnifies and focuses the light, projecting an upside down arrow.

MAKE A REFRACTING TELESCOPE

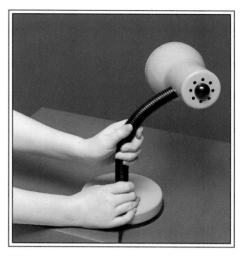

1 Trace around the head of the desk lamp on a sheet of red paper. Using scissors, cut out a star in the middle of the circle. Then cut out the circle, as shown.

2 Using tape, fasten the circle of paper securely over the front of the desk lamp. Make sure that it does not touch the bulb, as this could cause the paper to burn.

3 Position the desk lamp so that it shines on a nearby wall. Adjust the angle of the lamp if necessary. Make sure that the lamp's base is stable to prevent it from tipping.

You will need: desk lamp, thick red paper, marker, scissors, tape, 2 magnifying glasses, modeling clay.

Starlight   *Focal point*   *Eyepiece lens*

Objective lens

Refracting telescope
Light from a distant star passes through the objective lens. This forms a magnified, blurry image of the star. The image is brought into focus by the lens in the eyepiece.

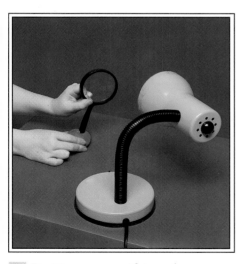

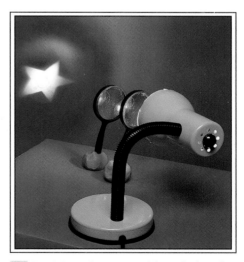

4 Position a magnifying glass between the lamp and the wall. To support the glass and attach it in place, take the handle and wedge it firmly in a lump of modeling clay.

5 Turn on the lamp. Adjust the magnifying glass so that the light passing through it appears as a blurred patch of light. The glass acts like a telescope's objective lens.

6 Position the second lens behind the first lens. This acts as an eyepiece lens. Adjust the eyepiece lens until the light is focused to form the sharp image of the star.

ROCKET PROPULSION

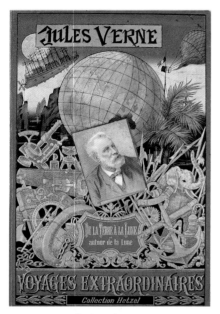

Visions of the future
In the late 1800s, the French writer Jules Verne (1828–1905) wrote imaginative stories about the future. He predicted space travel many years before the first aircraft flew in 1903.

ROCKET engines are the only motors powerful enough to lift a heavy spacecraft into orbit and beyond. The earliest rocket propulsion worked by burning a solid fuel. This type of rocket is not suitable for spaceflight because it cannot be controlled—the fuel simply burns until there is none left. Solid fuel booster rockets are used to help provide extra power during the liftoff of the space shuttle and the launch of some modern rockets. For spaceflight itself, a controllable rocket is usually needed. This type of engine can be turned on and off and varied in power like the engine of a car. Liquid fuel rockets are used for spaceflight as they can be controlled in this way. They produce a stream of searing hot gas from the engine nozzle, usually by burning a mixture of liquefied oxygen and liquid hydrogen fuel in a combustion chamber. The gases rushing out in one direction create a huge amount of thrust, pushing the rocket in the opposite direction. Spacecraft carry a supply of liquid oxygen on board as well as liquid fuel to enable their rockets to function in the airless environment of space.

Father of rocketry
A Russian schoolteacher named Konstantin Tsiolkovsky was the first person to develop written theories on rocket-powered space travel. He proposed the use of multi-stage rockets and liquid fuel. His ideas were first published in 1903.

Rocket weapon
A V-2 rocket blasts off during the 1940s. It was the world's first supersonic guided missile. The weapon was developed in Germany during the Second World War (1939-45). One of its designers, Wernher von Braun, joined the U.S. space program after the war. He later headed the design team for the Saturn 5 rocket, which took astronauts to the moon.

Liquid fuel rocket
American engineer Robert Goddard prepares to launch the world's first rocket propelled by a liquid fuel. Goddard's rocket was launched in 1926. Before this all rockets had been propelled by burning a solid fuel. Goddard's rocket soared to a height of 184 feet at a speed of almost 62 mph.

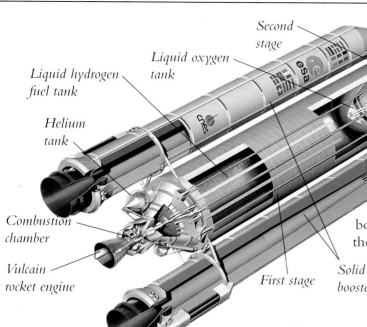

Second stage

Payload

Liquid oxygen tank

Liquid hydrogen fuel tank

Helium tank

Combustion chamber

Vulcain rocket engine

First stage

Solid rocket boosters

Inside Ariane 5

This illustration shows the inner workings of an Ariane 5 rocket, one of the largest launch vehicles of the European Space Agency's Ariane series. The Ariane rockets have launched many of the world's science and communications satellites. Ariane 5 is made of two rocket stages stacked on top of each other, with the payload housed in the nose cone. Two solid rocket boosters attached to the main body provide extra thrust. Each stage and both boosters are jettisoned (discarded) once they have used up their fuel. This reduces the weight of the rocket as it ascends.

Nose cone contains satellite payload

Ariane 5 launch sequence

Ready for launch

An Ariane 5 launch vehicle stands on its pad ready for liftoff. The rocket's nose cone contains two satellites, which it will launch into geostationary orbit around the Earth. Ariane 5 spacecraft can carry satellites with a mass up to 6.8 tons into space.

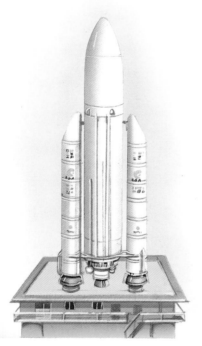

Launch

Liftoff! The main stage of the Ariane 5 burns about 130 tons of liquid hydrogen and 26 tons of liquid oxygen. Each of the booster rockets burns 237 tons of solid fuel as the Ariane 5 soars through the atmosphere.

Booster separation

At a height of 34 miles, only 129 seconds after liftoff, the two solid rocket boosters have exhausted their fuel supply. The rocket boosters are then jettisoned from the main body of the Ariane 5 vehicle.

Launching a satellite

At a height of 68 miles, the nose cone fairing of the Ariane 5 is jettisoned. The small second stage then carries the two satellites up into orbit. Finally, they are released into space.

ESCAPING FROM EARTH

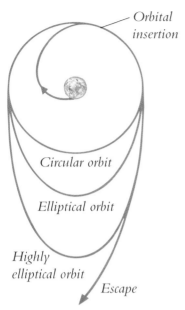

Orbital insertion

Circular orbit

Elliptical orbit

Highly elliptical orbit

Escape

T HE function of a rocket designed for spaceflight is to carry a satellite or astronauts into space. In order to do that, it has to overcome gravity (the force that pulls everything down to Earth). If the rocket's engines are not powerful enough, gravity will win and pull the rocket and its payload back to Earth. With more powerful engines, the rocket's attempt to fly into space is exactly equalled by the pull of gravity. With these two forces in perfect balance, a spacecraft will continue to circle the Earth. If the rocket is more powerful, it can fly fast enough to escape from Earth's gravity altogether and fly toward the moon or the planets. The speed that it needs to reach to do this is called escape velocity. You can demonstrate the speeds needed for escape velocity by trying out a simple experiment using a magnet and ball bearings. Then try launching your own cork model rocket from a plastic bottle.

Escape velocity

To go into orbit around the Earth, a spacecraft must reach a velocity of at least 17,700 mph. Depending on how fast it is travelling, the spacecraft may go into a circular, elliptical, or highly elliptical orbit. If it reaches a velocity of 25,000 mph, the spacecraft escapes from the Earth's gravity altogether.

LAUNCH A CHEMICAL ROCKET

You will need: baking soda, paper towel, water, vinegar, 2-liter plastic bottle, paper streamers, cork, push pin.

A chemical reaction between the vinegar (representing liquid oxygen) and baking soda (representing fuel) produces carbon dioxide gas. The gas pressure inside the bottle pushes against the cork. The cork is blasted into the air like a rocket lifting off.

1 Place a teaspoon of baking soda directly in the middle of a 4 x 8-inch piece of paper towel. Roll up the towel and twist the ends to keep the baking soda fuel inside.

2 Pour half a cup of water and the same amount of vinegar into the bottle. Fix paper streamers to the top of the cork with a push pin. Drop the towel inside.

3 Push the cork in immediately so that it is a snug fit, but not too tight. Quickly take the bottle outside. Then move at least 10 feet away from it and watch what happens.

ESCAPING FROM GRAVITY

You will need: thin card stock, ruler, pencil, scissors, magnetic strip, 4 x 2-inch piece of plastic, baking tray, modeling clay, tape, small steel ball bearings.

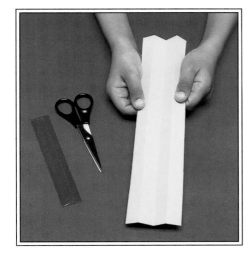

1 Measure out a 12 x 4-inch strip of thin card stock using a ruler. Cut it out with the scissors. Fold it lengthways into three sections to form an M-shaped trough.

2 Cut the magnetic strip into 5 short pieces. Glue these short strips to the plastic base to make a large, square bar magnet, as shown above.

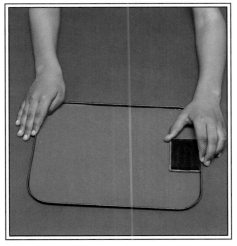

3 Fix the magnet firmly to one end of the tray with some of the modeling clay. Position it roughly in the middle. The magnet simulates the pull of the Earth's gravity.

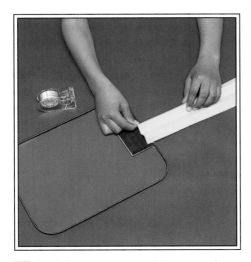

4 Position one end of the trough over the edge of the magnet. Attach it to the magnet with tape. The trough represents the path of a rocket as it ascends into orbit.

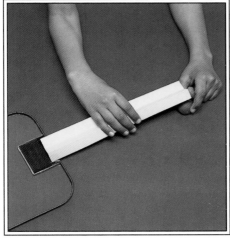

5 Roll the remaining modeling clay into a round ball. Position the clay ball underneath the other end of the M-shaped trough. This raises the trough at a slight angle.

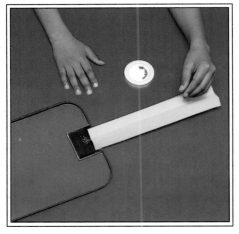

6 Place a small ball bearing at the end of the trough and let it roll down. The ball bearing sticks to the magnet. The velocity of the ball-bearing rocket along the trough's flight path is not fast enough to escape the pull of the magnet.

Ball bearing escapes the pull of the magnet

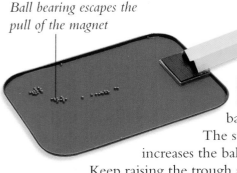

7 Raise the trough and roll another ball bearing along it. The steeper angle increases the ball bearing's velocity. Keep raising the trough and rolling ball bearings until one shoots past the magnet. It has then achieved escape velocity!

THE FIRST SPACE FLIGHTS

AFTER the Second World War (1939-45), the United States and the Soviet Union raced each other to build a rocket powerful enough to reach space. On October 4, 1957, the world learned that the Soviet Union had won the race. It had successfully placed the first artificial satellite, *Sputnik 1*, in orbit. Getting a satellite of any sort into space successfully was an achievement because rocket launchers often failed. They frequently blew up or flew off course. As these early liquid fuel rockets were not very powerful, the first satellites had to be very small and simple. But soon, larger and more reliable rockets were built. They could launch bigger, heavier satellites. These satellites were designed to do different jobs. Weather satellites made weather forecasts more accurate, while science satellites carried out scientific research. Communications satellites relayed telephone calls and television programs around the world, and Earth resources satellites studied the planet. The space age had begun.

Artificial satellite
The first artificial satellite, *Sputnik 1*, was a metal sphere measuring 23 inches and weighing 185 pounds. Its radio transmitter sent a signal to Earth for 21 days. After 96 days the satellite re-entered the atmosphere and burned up.

V2 technology
A modified V2 blasts off from an American launch pad in 1950. V2 rockets captured in Germany during the Second World War were taken to America. They were used to develop rockets for the U.S. space program.

Chimp in space
Ham the chimpanzee was launched into space on January 31st 1961. His mission was to test the safety of the Mercury capsule, which would be used to carry the first American astronaut into space. Ham survived his flight, proving the capsule was safe for humans.

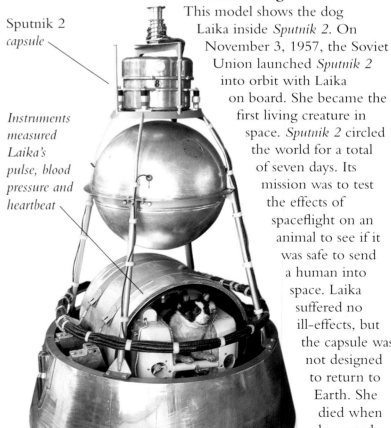

Sputnik 2 *capsule*

Instruments measured Laika's pulse, blood pressure and heartbeat

Animal testing
This model shows the dog Laika inside *Sputnik 2*. On November 3, 1957, the Soviet Union launched *Sputnik 2* into orbit with Laika on board. She became the first living creature in space. *Sputnik 2* circled the world for a total of seven days. Its mission was to test the effects of spaceflight on an animal to see if it was safe to send a human into space. Laika suffered no ill-effects, but the capsule was not designed to return to Earth. She died when her supply of oxygen ran out.

A TIROS satellite sits on top of a launch vehicle as it is fuelled for liftoff. A total of 10 TIROS satellites were launched between 1960 and 1965. They were the first weather satellites. Each TIROS satellite took 16 photographs of the Earth on every orbit. The photographs were then transmitted to Earth by radio when a ground receiving station came within range. The name TIROS stands for Television and Infra-Red Observation Satellite.

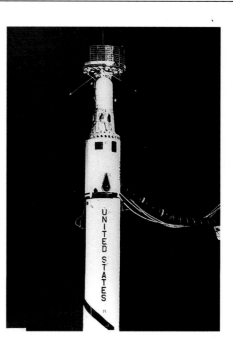

Explorer 1

The United States' first satellite, *Explorer 1*, clears the launch pad on January 31st 1958. The satellite's onboard instruments detected belts of intense radiation around the Earth. They were named the Van Allen belts, after the scientist who analyzed the satellite's data.

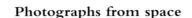

Photographs from space

The satellite *Explorer 6* was launched on August 7, 1959. It sent back the first photograph of the Earth taken from space. For the first time in the history of humanity, people were finally able to see their homes as one world. More than 50 Explorer satellites were launched over the next 16 years, providing scientists with a great deal of valuable information about space and the sun.

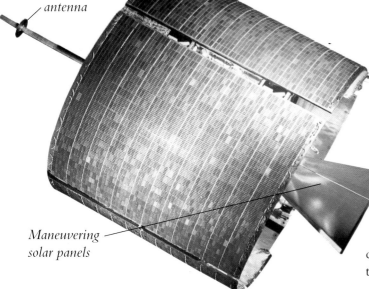

Radio antenna

Maneuvering solar panels

Early Bird

The first privately owned communications satellite, or comsat, was called *Early Bird*. The satellite was also known as *Intelsat 1*. The orbiting spacecraft could be used to relay up to a maximum of 240 telephone calls or one television channel. *Early Bird* revolutionized international communications as it provided a regular service for the transmission of television pictures across the Atlantic Ocean.

PEOPLE IN SPACE

Shielding protects capsule against heat of re-entry

THE human exploration of space began with Yury Gagarin's historic flight in *Vostok 1* in 1961. The Soviet cosmonaut made one orbit of the Earth. The United States entered the space race soon afterwards with its Mercury space project. These early spaceflights proved that human beings could travel into space and return safely to Earth. After six Vostok flights and six Mercury flights, both nations moved on to the next stage of their space programs. Soviet Voshkod flights achieved the first three-person flight and the first space walk, by Alexei Leonov. The United States launched 10 flights of the two-person Gemini spacecraft. These missions tried out all the maneuvers needed for a moon landing. Gemini astronauts learned how to locate other spacecraft, move towards them and dock (link up) with them. They also stayed in space for long periods, with the *Gemini 7* flight in 1965 lasting for a record 14 days. By the end of the Project Gemini flights, the U.S. was ready to send astronauts to the moon.

Vostok 1

The *Vostok 1* space capsule was an 8-foot wide sphere. For most of its flight, the capsule was attached to an instrument cylinder and rocket engine. The engine slowed the capsule to begin its descent from orbit and re-entry into the atmosphere.

Space pioneers

On April 12, 1961, the Soviet pilot Yury Gagarin became the first man to fly into space. Valentina Tereshkova became the first woman in space on June 16, 1963. Her flight in *Vostok 6* lasted 70 hours.

The Mercury Seven

The seven original Mercury astronauts show off their new silver spacesuits. Alan Shepard became the first American in space on May 5, 1961. His Mercury capsule was fired up into space and dropped back immediately to Earth without going into orbit. John Glenn became the first American to orbit the Earth nine months later. Glenn did not go into space again until his historic flight aboard the space shuttle in 1998.

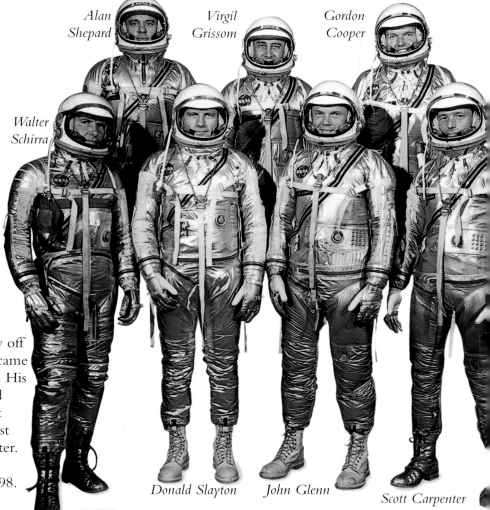

Alan Shepard *Virgil Grissom* *Gordon Cooper*

Walter Schirra

Donald Slayton *John Glenn* *Scott Carpenter*

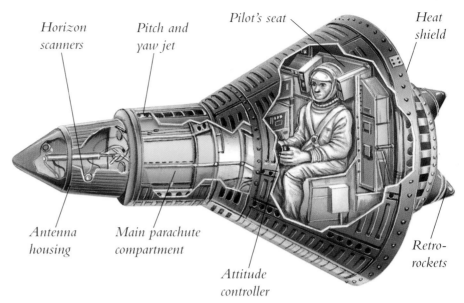

Horizon scanners

Pitch and yaw jet

Pilot's seat

Heat shield

Antenna housing

Main parachute compartment

Attitude controller

Retro-rockets

Inside a Mercury capsule

The Mercury capsule was tiny. It measured 9½ feet from top to bottom and about 6 feet across the heat shield. The astronaut lay in the spacecraft with his back to the shield. The capsule's narrow nose housed the parachutes that slowed its descent through the atmosphere before splashdown.

Friendship 7

John Glenn's Mercury capsule rises off the launch pad atop an Atlas rocket on February 20, 1962. The capsule, named *Friendship 7*, orbited the Earth for more than four hours, before splashing down into the sea.

Walking in space

Ed White floats in space, connected to his space capsule by a thin tether. The 1965 *Gemini 4* flight saw White become the first U.S. astronaut to perform a spacewalk.

Gemini splashdown

David Scott and Neil Armstrong breathe a sigh of relief in their *Gemini 8* capsule after splashdown. The 1966 mission almost ended in disaster. The astronauts only regained control after a faulty thruster made the craft spin wildly. Armstrong later became the first person to walk on the moon.

MOON MISSION

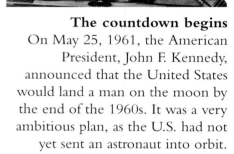

THE 50-ton Apollo spacecraft needed the world's most powerful rocket, the Saturn 5, to send it to the moon and back. The Apollo spacecraft was made in three parts—the command module (CM), the service module (SM) and the lunar excursion module (LEM). The three-man crew lived in the tiny command module for the three-day flight to the moon and for another three days on the return journey. The service module attached to it provided electricity and air to breathe. The lunar module was the strange, spider-like craft used to make the moon landing. First, the Apollo spacecraft was checked out in Earth orbit by the *Apollo 7* mission. In December 1968, *Apollo 8* travelled to the moon, swung around behind it and returned to Earth. Two more practice missions followed. Then, in July 1969, *Apollo 11* made history by landing astronauts on the moon for the first time.

The countdown begins
On May 25, 1961, the American President, John F. Kennedy, announced that the United States would land a man on the moon by the end of the 1960s. It was a very ambitious plan, as the U.S. had not yet sent an astronaut into orbit.

***Apollo 11* crew**
Neil Armstrong, Michael Collins and Edwin (Buzz) Aldrin were selected to be the first Apollo crew to land on the moon. Armstrong was chosen as mission commander, in overall control of the spacecraft and crew. Aldrin had the job of flying the lunar excursion module (LEM). Collins was the command/service module (CSM) pilot, and remained in orbit while Armstrong and Aldrin walked on the surface of the moon.

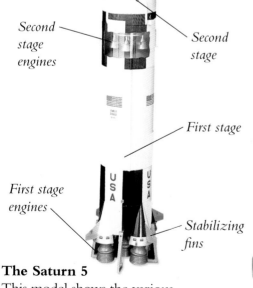

Command module (CM)
Service module (SM)
Lunar excursion module (LEM)
Instrument unit
Third stage
Third stage engine
Second stage engines
Second stage
First stage
First stage engines
Stabilizing fins

The Saturn 5
This model shows the various components of the Saturn 5 launch vehicle. Its three rocket stages were jettisoned in turn as they used up their fuel. Only the third stage and the Apollo spacecraft modules reached the moon.

Michael Collins

Neil Armstrong

Edwin (Buzz) Aldrin

Crawler transporter
The Saturn 5 rocket and Apollo spacecraft roll slowly from the assembly building to the launch pad on top of a crawler transporter. This strange vehicle weighed 3,000 tons and needed a crew of 15 to operate it.

Liftoff!
The *Apollo 11* mission gets underway as the mighty Saturn 5 rises off the launch pad. The escape tower on the top of the rocket was jettisoned once the Saturn 5 was safely in flight. The enormous power of its five first-stage engines made the ground beneath the Saturn 5 shake like an earthquake. The rocket was driven up by the rush of hot exhaust gases from the engines. Exhaust from four of the first-stage engines balanced the weight of the 3,000-ton rocket as the fifth engine provided the thrust required for liftoff.

Approaching the moon
The *Apollo 11* lunar module, called the *Eagle*, drops out of lunar orbit and heads for its landing site. The date is July 20, 1969. Inside it are Neil Armstrong and Buzz Aldrin. Shortly after touchdown, Neil Armstrong descends the lunar module ladder. As he places his foot on the lunar soil he says "That's one small step for a man —one giant leap for mankind."

Stepping out
Buzz Aldrin descends the *Eagle*'s ladder, becoming the second astronaut to walk on the moon. His spacesuit's Portable Life Support System (PLSS) backpack is clearly visible as he lowers himself down. As he looks around at the moon's lifeless surface, Aldrin describes the view as "magnificent desolation."

FACT BOX

• The distance between the Earth and the moon is about 238,900 miles.

• During the lunar day the moon's surface temperature can be as high as 248°F. At night, the temperature is as low as -227.2°F.

• The moon completes one full orbit of the Earth every 271/2 days.

GOING TO THE MOON

PLOTTING a course to the moon is not as easy as travelling from place to place on a planet's surface. On Earth, people can navigate by following landmarks or natural features, such as hills, valleys and rivers. Pilots who fly at high altitudes navigate by using radio beacons on the ground or signals from satellites. The problem with travelling from the Earth to the moon is that both are moving. If you take off from the Earth with your spacecraft aimed directly at the moon, it will not be there by the time you arrive. The moon will have moved on around its orbit. If you aim at the moon and continually change your direction to follow its movements, you will use an enormous amount of fuel. The answer is to aim your spacecraft at the place where the moon will be by the time you get there. However, you also need to make sure you are not drifting off course on the way. Spacecrafts use one of the oldest navigation methods. They navigate by the stars. Try your hand at aiming at a moving target by following this simple project. You can also demonstrate staging by making your own two-stage rocket.

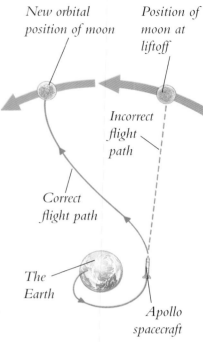

New orbital position of moon *Position of moon at liftoff*

Incorrect flight path

Correct flight path

The Earth

Apollo spacecraft

Moving targets
This diagram shows two possible flight paths for an Apollo spacecraft. Aiming directly at the moon does not take into account its movement as it orbits the Earth. The correct, efficient route compensates for the moon's orbital movement by aiming ahead of its position at liftoff.

AIMING AT THE MOON

You will need: string, ruler, scissors, masking tape, metal washer, book, small balls of paper.

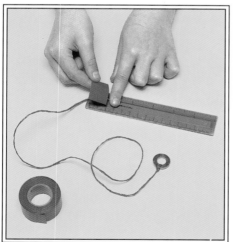

1 Measure out 24 inches of string with the ruler. Cut it off with scissors. Tape one end of the string to one end of the ruler. Tie a washer to the other end of the string.

2 Place the ruler on a table or box with the string hanging over the edge. Weigh it down with a heavy book. Try hitting the washer by throwing small balls of paper at it.

3 Start the washer swinging and try to hit it again with the paper balls. See how much more difficult it is to hit a moving target, like a spacecraft aiming at a moving moon.

MAKE A TWO-STAGE ROCKET

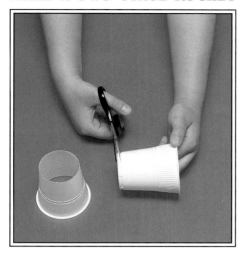

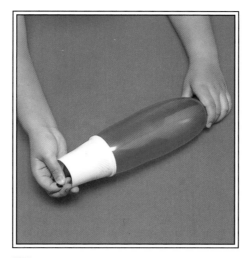

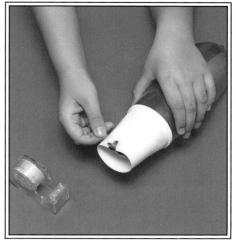

1 Using scissors, carefully cut the bottom out of a paper or plastic cup. This will serve as the linking collar between the two stages of the balloon rocket.

2 Partly blow up the long balloon with the balloon pump. Pull its neck through the paper cup. This balloon will be your two-stage rocket's second stage.

3 Fold the neck of the long balloon over the side of the cup. Tape the end of the balloon's neck to the cup to stop the air from escaping, as shown.

You will need: 2 paper or plastic cups, scissors, long balloon, balloon pump, tape, round balloon.

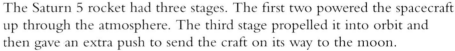

Second stage fires

First stage jettisoned

Second stage jettisoned

Third stage fires

Third stage powers command/service module (CSM) towards the moon

Rocket staging

The Saturn 5 rocket had three stages. The first two powered the spacecraft up through the atmosphere. The third stage propelled it into orbit and then gave an extra push to send the craft on its way to the moon.

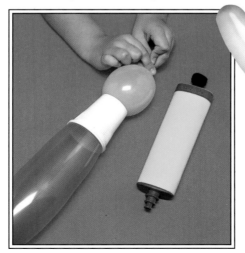

4 Carefully push the round balloon into the open end of the paper or plastic cup. This balloon will form the first stage of your two-stage balloon rocket.

5 Blow up the round balloon so that it wedges the neck of the long balloon in place inside the cup. Hold the neck of the round balloon to keep the air inside it.

6 Peel the tape off the neck of the long balloon. Hold the rocket as shown. Let go of the round balloon's neck. Air rushes out, launching the first stage of the rocket. It then falls, launching the second stage balloon.

EXPLORING THE MOON

APOLLO astronauts explored the moon in two ways. On the earlier missions they walked on the surface in the area around the lunar module. On later trips, they also drove around in the lunar roving vehicle (LRV). They collected rock samples and laid out scientific instruments on the lunar surface. The instruments continued to send information about the moon back to scientists on Earth after the astronauts left. To return to Earth, the upper part of the lunar module blasted off, using the base as a launch pad. It then docked with the command/service module (CSM). With all three astronauts on board the CSM again, the lunar module was jettisoned. The service module's rocket engine fired and set the CSM on course for the Earth. Once in orbit, the command module separated from the service module for re-entry. Inside the atmosphere, parachutes slowed the capsule's descent before splashdown in the Pacific Ocean.

Man on the moon
This famous photograph of Buzz Aldrin was taken by Neil Armstrong. If you look very closely, you can see Armstrong and the lunar module reflected in Aldrin's helmet visor.

Footprints in the dust
The Apollo astronauts left behind many footprints and impressions in the lunar dust. They will still be there millions of years from now. Unlike the Earth, there is no wind on the moon to disturb the footprints or rain to wash them away.

Jumping on the moon
The moon's pull of gravity is one-sixth of that of the Earth. This means you could jump six times farther and higher on the moon than on Earth. You can demonstrate this by trying out a simple experiment. Lay a string in a straight line on the ground. Stand on one side of the string with your toes touching it. Jump as far as you can over the string. Ask someone to measure the distance from the string to where you landed. Multiply this by six to find out how far you could jump on the moon.

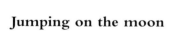

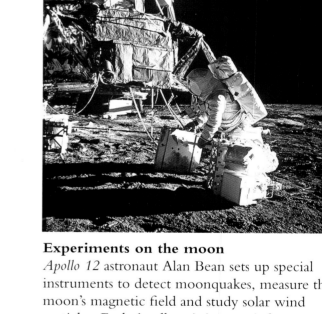

Experiments on the moon
Apollo 12 astronaut Alan Bean sets up special instruments to detect moonquakes, measure the moon's magnetic field and study solar wind particles. Each Apollo mission carried out a variety of different scientific experiments.

FACT BOX

• The moon's gravitational pull on the Earth is the main cause of the regular rise and fall of the tides in our planet's many oceans and seas.

Apollo 13

Fred Haise, Jack Swigert and James Lovell were the crew members of the ill-fated *Apollo 13* mission in 1971. An explosion inside the spacecraft's service module about 205,000 miles from Earth nearly left the crew marooned in space. Tens of thousands of technicians on Earth worked around the clock to help the crew bring their damaged spacecraft safely home.

Lunar rover

Apollo 17 astronaut Eugene Cernan takes the lunar roving vehicle for a drive in the Taurus-Littrow region of the moon. This small electric car was carried on the final three Apollo moon missions (*Apollo 15, 16* and *17*). The vehicle enabled astronauts to travel further and collect more rock samples from a wider area.

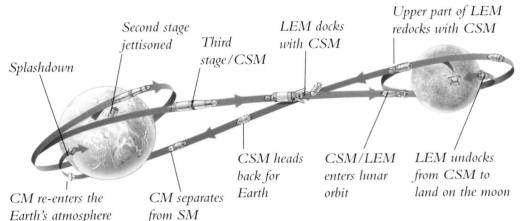

Upper part of LEM redocks with CSM

LEM docks with CSM

Second stage jettisoned

Third stage/CSM

Splashdown

CM re-enters the Earth's atmosphere

CM separates from SM

CSM heads back for Earth

CSM/LEM enters lunar orbit

LEM undocks from CSM to land on the moon

An Apollo mission

This illustration shows the various stages of an Apollo moon mission. One of the most dangerous stages was re-entry into the Earth's atmosphere. The command module had to hit the atmosphere at exactly the right angle. Too shallow an angle would cause the spacecraft to bounce back into space. Too steep an angle would cause it to burn up in the Earth's atmosphere.

Splashdown

The *Apollo 17* command module splashes down in the Pacific Ocean. After a high speed re-entry into the atmosphere, the capsule floats slowly down under three huge parachutes. Splashdown marked the end of an Apollo mission. Recovery crews waiting in nearby ships rushed to the spacecraft to help the astronauts out of the capsule.

LIVING IN SPACE

Controlling moisture
Place a lamp by a glass jar so its heat makes water at the bottom of the jar evaporate. The jar's cooler sides cause the vapor to condense back into water. Heat from the sun makes this happen inside a spacesuit too, but the suit's systems remove the moisture.

THE human body evolved over millions of years to live on the surface of the Earth. It is totally unsuited to living in space, where there is no air, little gravity and it is freezing cold in the shade and roasting hot in direct sunshine. Astronauts have to take Earth-like conditions with them into space. They need air to breathe, warmth, food, water and light. They also require radio equipment to keep in touch with each other and with mission controllers on Earth. Life support systems and communications equipment all need electricity, so they have to take an electricity generator with them too. The human body is very good at changing to suit the conditions around it. During long space missions, these changes can become a problem. Without gravity to work against, muscles waste away and bones lose calcium. To stay healthy, astronauts exercise using special machines.

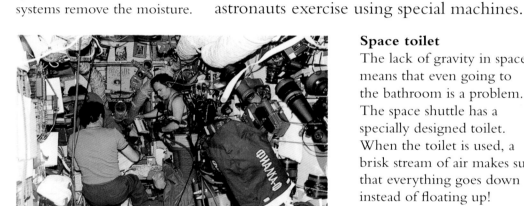

Space toilet
The lack of gravity in space means that even going to the bathroom is a problem. The space shuttle has a specially designed toilet. When the toilet is used, a brisk stream of air makes sure that everything goes down instead of floating up!

Life on Mir
Crew members aboard the Russian space station *Mir* test the effects of living in space on the body. Russian cosmonauts and American astronauts have lived aboard *Mir* for long periods, some for more than a year at a time.

Space meals
Most food on board the space shuttle is dehydrated. To prepare it, hot or cold water is added. Some foods, such as beef and ham, are prepared in an oven in the usual way.

Keeping fit
Astronaut Richard M. Linnehan performs his daily workout aboard the space shuttle *Columbia*. Daily exercise is essential for keeping healthy in space. An astronaut has to have some resistance to work against, to prevent his or her muscles wasting away. On the shuttle, resistance is provided by pulling down on elastic straps or springs. Toe straps anchor the weightless astronaut securely to the deck.

Extra-Vehicular Activity

Astronauts often have to work outside their space station or spacecraft. This is referred to as Extra-Vehicular Activity (EVA). Space shuttle astronauts may have to prepare a satellite for launch or operate a scientific experiment. They wear spacesuits with life-support backpacks that enable them to survive in the harsh environment of space. Here they are working in the shuttle's payload bay. The astronauts are clipped to lifelines that stop them from floating away into space.

Dressing for space

A space shuttle astronaut prepares for her Extra-Vehicular Activity (EVA), or spacewalk. First she puts on a liquid-cooling and ventilation garment. Cool water pumped through a network of tubing stops the astronaut from overheating in space. Next, she steps into the spacesuit legs and lower body. Then she wriggles up inside the suit's upper body and locks the two suit halves together. The astronaut then puts on a radio headset. Finally, the helmet and gloves are locked into place.

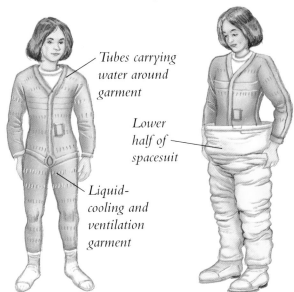

Tubes carrying water around garment

Lower half of spacesuit

Liquid-cooling and ventilation garment

Upper half of space suit

Locking ring

Lower half of space suit

Radio headset

Helmet

Gloves

Sleeping in zero-gravity

A space shuttle astronaut dozes in a sleep restraint on board the space shuttle *Columbia*. The restraint is necessary to stop the astronaut from floating around the cabin as he rests. The design of the sleep restraint is very similar to that of an ordinary zip-up sleeping bag. It can be used in many locations inside the Orbiter crew compartment.

FACT BOX

• On early spaceflights, spacesuits were custom-made for each astronaut. Space shuttle astronauts now wear standard spacesuits that are made in a range of sizes.

• Russian cosmonaut Valeriy Poliyakov holds the record for the longest continuous period of time spent in space. He stayed on board the *Mir* space station for a total of 437 consecutive days.

SPACE SHUTTLE

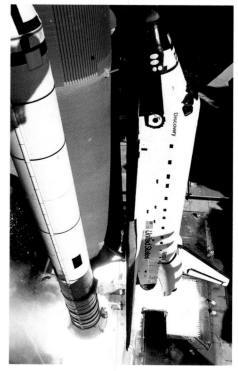

FOR the first 24 years of the space age, every rocket and spacecraft was custom designed for one mission only. Nothing was used a second time. This was an extremely costly and wasteful method of going into space. Scientists realized that if spaceflight was to become as common as other ways of travelling, spacecraft must be reusable, like aircraft or ships. The world's first reusable spacecraft, the United States' space shuttle Orbiter, was launched for the first time on April 12, 1981. The space shuttle Orbiter is a space plane. It is about the same size as a small airliner. The spacecraft is designed to take off like a rocket, complete its mission in space, return to Earth and land on a runway like an aircraft. Its short, stubby wings help it to glide down through the atmosphere. The U.S. Orbiter also has a large payload bay. It is used for carrying satellites or other structures into space or for bringing them back to Earth for repair. A similar spacecraft was developed by the Soviet Union in the 1980s, but it only made one orbital flight.

Shuttle transporter
The space shuttle is carried on the same crawler transporter that moved Saturn 5 rockets from the assembly building to the launch pad. Each Shuttle will make this journey many times during its working life.

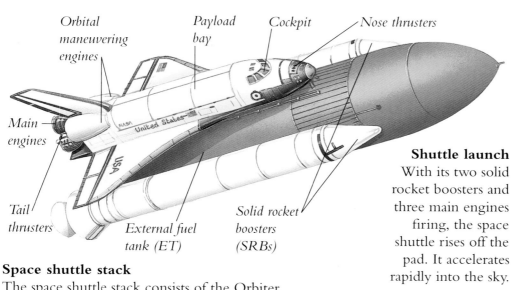

Orbital maneuvering engines

Payload bay

Cockpit

Nose thrusters

Main engines

Tail thrusters

External fuel tank (ET)

Solid rocket boosters (SRBs)

Shuttle launch
With its two solid rocket boosters and three main engines firing, the space shuttle rises off the pad. It accelerates rapidly into the sky.

Space shuttle stack
The space shuttle stack consists of the Orbiter, an external fuel tank (ET) and two solid rocket boosters (SRBs). The Orbiter is attached to the giant external fuel tank, which supplies its three main engines with liquid hydrogen fuel and liquid oxygen during the launch. The SRBs are attached to either side of the ET to provide extra takeoff power. In space, smaller orbital maneuvering engines take over. Even smaller thrusters in the nose and tail are used to make adjustments to the Orbiter's position.

Shuttle cockpit
The space shuttle is flown by the mission commander and pilot, who sit on the flight deck in the Orbiter's nose. They are surrounded by control panels and computer screens.

Lifting bodies

The HL–10 aircraft *(below)* is a lifting body, one a series of test vehicles built before the Orbiter was designed. Lifting bodies were designed to test how a vehicle with very short wings would fly. This shape was chosen as it would survive the heat of re-entry and could also be flown like a plane inside the atmosphere.

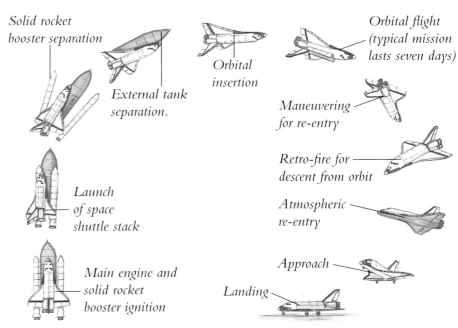

The X–15

During the 1960s, long before the space shuttle was built, another rocket plane was flying to the fringes of the atmosphere. The X-15 was an experimental plane used to study flight at very great heights. Results from the X-15 test flights were used to help design and develop the space shuttle.

Shuttle mission profile

Two minutes after launch, at a height of 28 miles, the solid rocket boosters fall away. Six minutes later, the main engines shut down and the external tank is jettisoned. The orbital maneuvering engines then fire twice to insert the Orbiter in orbit about 250 miles above the Earth. When the mission is completed, the Orbiter maneuveres for re-entry. It fires its orbital engines to slow it down (retro-fire), and then begins its descent. After re-entry, the shuttle glides to a landing, usually touching down at the Kennedy Space Center in Florida.

Solid rocket booster separation

External tank separation.

Launch of space shuttle stack

Main engine and solid rocket booster ignition

Orbital insertion

Orbital flight (typical mission lasts seven days)

Maneuvering for re-entry

Retro-fire for descent from orbit

Atmospheric re-entry

Approach

Landing

Human spacecraft

Astronaut Bruce McCandless floats above the payload bay. He is wearing the manned maneuvering unit (MMU), a gas-powered jetpack that allows him to maneuver in space independently from the shuttle.

Soviet shuttle

This is the *Buran* shuttle built by the Soviet Union during the 1980s. Like the U.S. Orbiter, *Buran* was protected from the searing heat of re-entry by glassy silica tiles and fireproof cloth. The Soviet shuttle was only launched into space once, completing two orbits of the Earth in November 1988. *Buran* did not carry a crew on its flight and returned to Earth under automatic control.

WORKING IN SPACE

Working in a spacesuit
Bulky spacesuits make working in space difficult. Spacesuit designers are always trying to improve them. The more flexible a suit is, the less tiring it is to work in. This in turn enables an astronaut to work outside for longer periods.

WORKING inside the pressurized crew-compartment of the space shuttle is a little more difficult than on Earth because there is no gravity. On Earth, gravity pulls us down and also gives us something to push against. If a weightless astronaut pushes a handle in zero-gravity, the astronaut flies away in the opposite direction! This means that astronauts have to be anchored to something solid before they can do any work. Outside the space shuttle, a spacesuit makes it even more difficult to work. The astronaut has to work in the suit to make a fist or bend an arm or leg. Spacesuit gloves have thin rubber fingerpads so that astronauts can feel things through them, but they are still hard to work with. Simulate working in space by following an experiment using rubber gloves, a bowl of water and some nuts and bolts. Then try making a robot arm like the space shuttle's remote manipulator system (RMS), which is used to launch and retrieve satellites.

WORKING IN ZERO-GRAVITY

You will need: nuts and bolts, rubber gloves, bowl, water.

1 Take the nuts and bolts and place them on a table. Now pick them up and screw them together. You should find this a very easy task to achieve.

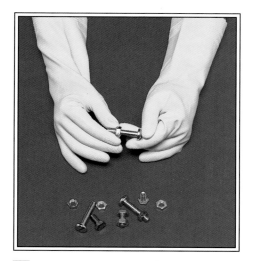

2 Now try screwing the nuts and bolts together with the gloves on. This is more difficult, like trying to carry out a delicate task on Earth wearing bulky spacesuit gloves.

3 Fill the bowl with water. Add the nuts and bolts. Try screwing them together with the gloves on. This is very difficult, like working in a spacesuit outside a spacecraft.

MAKE A ROBOT ARM

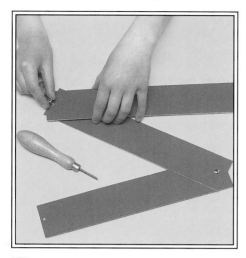

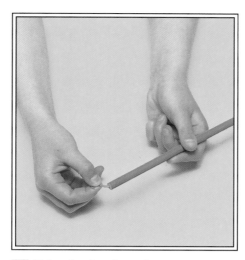

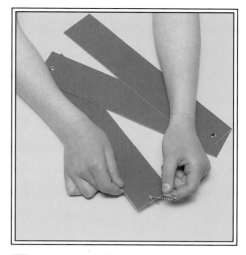

1 Use the ruler to measure out three 11 x 2-inch cardboard strips. Cut them out. Make a hole 1-inch from the end of each strip. Join the strips with paper fasteners, as shown.

2 Take the hook and screw it into the end of the dowel. The dowel will be used to remotely control the robot arm, just as Shuttle astronauts remotely operate the RMS.

3 Now carefully bend one of the paperclips into the shape of the letter S. To attach the paperclip, pass it through the hole in the end of the cardboard arm, as shown.

You will need: thick cardboard, ruler, scissors, awl, 2 paper fasteners, dowel, picture hook, 2 paper clips, ball of modeling clay.

Remote manipulator system
The space shuttle's RMS is controlled by an astronaut inside the Orbiter. Special tools attached to the end of the arm enable the RMS to retrieve faulty satellites and place them in the payload bay.

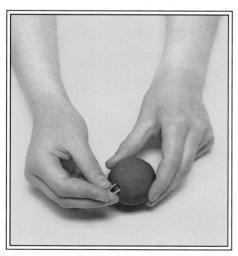

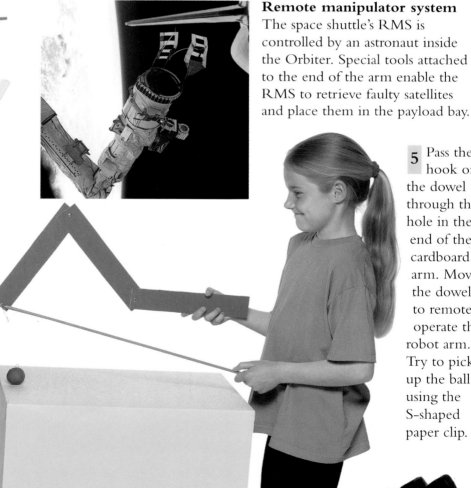

4 Take the modeling clay and roll it into a ball about the size of a walnut. Then take the second paperclip and push it firmly into the clay ball, as shown.

5 Pass the hook on the dowel through the hole in the end of the cardboard arm. Move the dowel to remotely operate the robot arm. Try to pick up the ball using the S-shaped paper clip.

SPACE STATIONS

A SPACE STATION IS a spacecraft that stays in orbit for its entire working life. A crew lives and works on board the station. The first, smallest space stations were launched into space in one piece. Later, larger stations were launched in pieces and put together in orbit. Space stations enable astronauts to carry out experiments lasting months or even years, and to make observations of the sun and the Earth over long periods. The first space station was the Soviet Union's *Salyut 1*, launched in 1971. It was the first of a series of Salyut stations, which ended with *Salyut 7*, launched in April 1982. The first American space station was *Skylab*, which was put into space in May 1973. Although it suffered serious damage during launch, the station was visited by three crews who lived and worked on board until February 1974. In February 1986, the Soviet Union launched the space station *Mir*. Extra parts have been added onto *Mir*, making it the biggest station yet constructed. A new, even larger International Space Station (ISS) is currently under development.

FACT BOX

• *Skylab* crews took a total of about 40,000 pictures of the Earth from space. The astronauts used up around 182,000 frames of film photographing the sun.

• The Russian space station *Mir* was badly damaged in June 1997 when an automated supply spacecraft crashed into it.

• *Skylab* re-entered the Earth's atmosphere in July 1979. Most of it burnt up and disintegrated on re-entry, but some parts of it fell on western Australia and into the Indian Ocean.

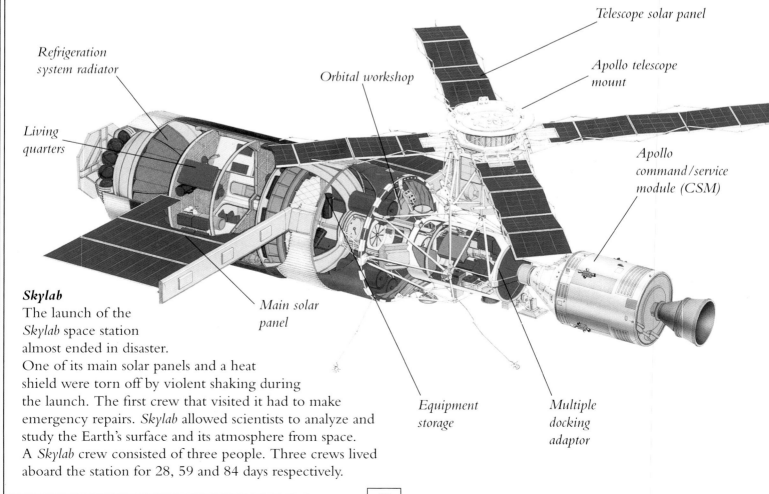

Telescope solar panel

Apollo telescope mount

Refrigeration system radiator

Orbital workshop

Apollo command/service module (CSM)

Living quarters

Skylab
The launch of the *Skylab* space station almost ended in disaster. One of its main solar panels and a heat shield were torn off by violent shaking during the launch. The first crew that visited it had to make emergency repairs. *Skylab* allowed scientists to analyze and study the Earth's surface and its atmosphere from space. A *Skylab* crew consisted of three people. Three crews lived aboard the station for 28, 59 and 84 days respectively.

Main solar panel

Equipment storage

Multiple docking adaptor

Salyut 7

The main body of *Salyut* 7 was about 42 feet long by 14 feet across and weighed 19 tons. The station had three main parts—a docking port for spacecraft to link up with it, a mid-section (equipped with a laboratory and living quarters) and a propulsion module.

Mir

The space station *Mir* has provided important information on the long-term effects of living in space. This will prove useful for future long-distance space missions, some of which may last for several years. The aging Russian station has suffered many breakdowns. Overcoming them has also provided valuable experience in operating spacecraft for long periods of time.

The Earth

Orbiting debris varies in size and shape

Space debris

Millions of pieces of debris orbit the Earth at high speed. Some are large, such as the discarded stages of old rockets. Other are tiny, such as paint fragments. Pieces fly in all directions and collide with other pieces, breaking them up into even smaller fragments. These fast-moving pieces of space junk are a hazard and can cause serious damage if they collide with an orbiting space vehicle or satellite.

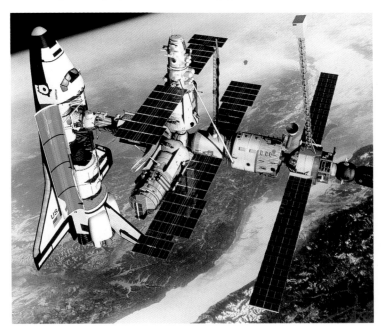

Shuttle docking

The space shuttle *Atlantis* docks with the Russian space station *Mir* in June 1995. It is using a docking adaptor made specially for the job. The space shuttle has docked with *Mir* several times, carrying visiting U.S. astronauts to live and work aboard the orbiting station.

ARTIFICIAL GRAVITY

Wheels in space
The film *2001: A Space Odyssey* featured a fictional rotating wheel-shaped space station. In theory, the centrifugal force generated by its rotation would create artificial gravity, holding people and objects against the walls of the wheel.

S PACE travellers in orbit or far away from Earth do not feel the pull of gravity. They feel weightless. In this state of weightlessness there is no up or down, because up and down are created by gravity. Even experienced pilots and astronauts sometimes feel uncomfortable or ill until they get used to being weightless. Weightlessness also has damaging effects on the human body. Future space stations and spacecraft designed for very long spaceflights may create artificial gravity to protect their occupants from the effects of weightlessness. One theoretical method of creating artificial gravity is to use rotation. Moving objects tend to travel in straight lines. When you whirl around a ball attached to the end of a piece of string, it tries to fly off in a straight line, stopped only by the string. Inside a rotating spacecraft, the solid outer walls would stop astronauts flying off in straight lines. The centrifugal force generated by the rotation would hold them against the outer walls, just as the Earth's gravity keeps us on the ground.

MAKE A CENTRIFUGE

You will need: 4 thick cardboard triangles (12 x 4 x 9 inches), dish washer liquid bottle, tape, awl, skewer, long rubber band, masking tape, 3 paper clips, pliers, thick cardboard (20 x 2 inches), 2 beads, drinking straw, 2 small plastic cups, modeling clay, water, food coloring.

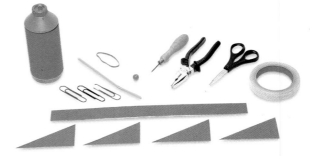

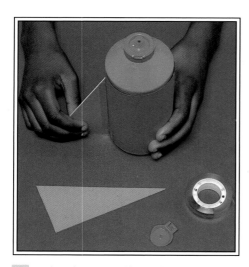

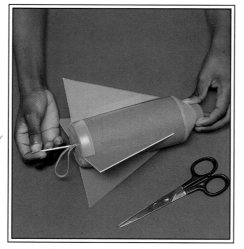

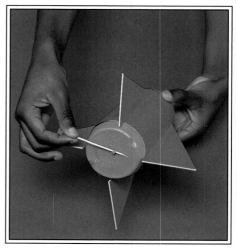

1 Take the 4 cardboard triangles and tape them to the sides of the bottle, as shown. These will provide the bottle centrifuge with a broad, stable base to stand on.

2 Using the awl, make a hole in the bottom of the bottle. Push one end of the rubber band nearly all the way into the hole using a short skewer.

3 Pass the skewer right through the small loop of rubber band projecting from the hole, as shown. Leave an equal amount of stick on either side of the bottle.

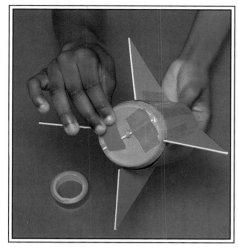

4 Take the masking tape and firmly secure the skewer to the base of the dishwashing liquid bottle. Make sure that the stick is fixed so tightly that it cannot move.

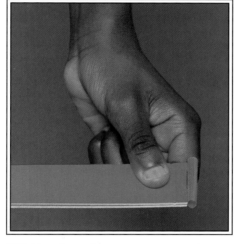

5 Straighten out one end of a paper clip with pliers. Dip the hooked end of the clip into the neck of the bottle. Catch the rubber band with the hook and pull it out.

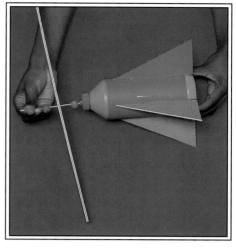

6 Using the scissors, make a hole in the middle of the 20 x 2-inch strip. Thread the end of the paper clip through the bead. Then thread it through the hole in the cardboard strip.

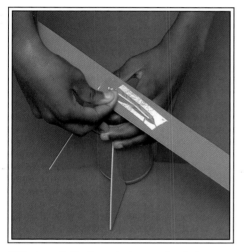

7 Carefully bend the end of the paper clip down onto the cardboard strip. Using tape, fix the end of the clip securely into place, as shown.

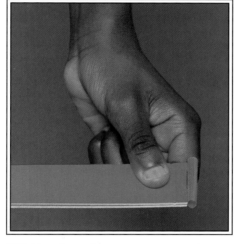

8 Use the scissors to cut two short pieces of drinking straw. Each piece should measure 2 inches in length. Fix one piece to each end of the cardboard strip with tape.

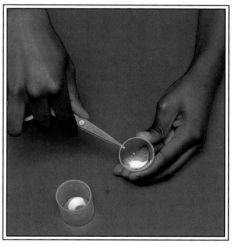

9 Take one of the small plastic cups. Make a hole with the scissors on either side of the cup near the top. Now make holes in the second cup in the same way.

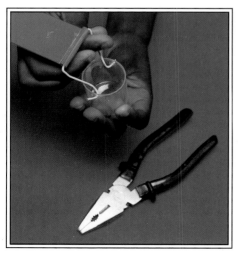

10 Straighten two paper clips with pliers. Thread a clip through each of the straws. Use the pliers to bend the ends of the clips down into hooks. Attach the cups by threading the ends of the clips through the holes, as shown. Make sure the cups can swing freely.

11 Stick the centrifuge to a flat surface with modeling clay. Fill the cups one-quarter full with water. Add food coloring to make the water show up clearly. Then turn the cardboard strip until the rubber band is wound up. Let the strip go and watch the cups as it spins around rapidly. The cups fly outward, but the water is held in place by centrifugal force.

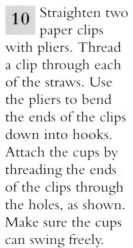

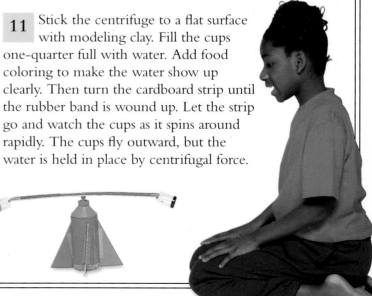

ROBOT EXPLORERS

Most of the solar system's planets are too far away from us to send astronauts to explore them. Instead, robot explorers are sent to be our eyes and ears in the distant reaches of the solar system. They have either landed on or flown past almost every planet in the solar system. On their travels, they have taken close-up photographs of the planets and their moons and taken measurements from their surfaces and atmospheres. *Luna 1* was the first space probe, heading out toward the moon in 1959. *Mariner* spacecraft then flew by Mercury, Venus and Mars. The *Venera* probes landed on the surface of Venus and the *Viking* landers touched down on Mars. The most widely travelled deep space probes are *Pioneer 10* and *11*, and *Voyager 1* and *2*, which have toured most of the solar system's outer planets. They used the pull of gravity from each planet they passed to change their course and speed them on their way to the next planet.

A message from Earth
Pioneer 10 carried a message from Earth to possible extraterrestrial life. Inscriptions on a metal plate fixed to the probe showed a man and a woman and the locations in space of the Earth and the sun.

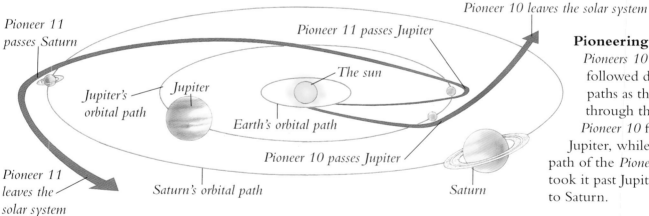

Pioneer 11 passes Saturn

Pioneer 11 passes Jupiter

Pioneer 10 leaves the solar system

Jupiter's orbital path

Jupiter

The sun

Earth's orbital path

Pioneer 10 passes Jupiter

Pioneer 11 leaves the solar system

Saturn's orbital path

Saturn

Pioneering probes
Pioneers 10 and *11* followed different flight paths as they travelled through the solar system. *Pioneer 10* flew past Jupiter, while the flight path of the *Pioneer 11* probe took it past Jupiter and then to Saturn.

Volcanic activity on Venus
This radar image was taken by the *Magellan* probe in orbit around the planet Venus. It shows Ushas Mons, a volcano in the southern hemisphere that rises 1¼ miles above the planet's surface. Lava flows stretch for hundreds of miles away from the volcano.

Neptune flyby
Voyager 2 flew past the distant planet Neptune in 1989. The images sent back by the probe revealed a strange, inhospitable world. The surface is completely hidden from view by a blue haze of methane gas, and high, wispy white clouds made from frozen hydrogen sulfide.

Sojourner

In 1997, the *Mars Pathfinder* lander released the six-wheeled *Sojourner* rover on the surface of Mars. It moved around carrying out tests for three months. The rover's exploratory mission ended when the lander's battery failed.

Testing rocks

Sojourner was controlled by radio signals from Earth. Its mission was to drive up to nearby rocks and carry out tests on them. It moved from rock to rock, using an X-ray spectrometer to test what substances they were made of.

Galileo mission

As the *Galileo* spacecraft approached Jupiter in 1995, it sent a probe into the gas giant's atmosphere. As the probe descended into the clouds, it began sending back information to the orbiter. The orbiter in turn relayed the data back to receivers on Earth. The *Galileo* probe continued to transmit its data about Jupiter for 57 minutes. It was then destroyed by heat and the intense atmospheric pressure of the gas giant.

Galileo *orbiter*

Galileo *probe separates from orbiter*

Magellan probe

The *Magellan* space probe went into orbit around Venus in 1990. Its mission was to map the planet's surface. Radar was used to reveal the surface features, as radio signals can pass through the thick clouds that hide the planet's surface from view.

Mission to Saturn

Cassini-Huygens is a two-part spacecraft that is currently on its way to the planet Saturn. When it arrives in 2004, the *Cassini* craft will orbit Saturn. The smaller *Huygens* probe will be sent to land on Saturn's giant moon, Titan.

SLINGSHOTS AND ANTENNAE

Pioneer *10* and *11*, *Voyager 1* and *2* and many other space probes used gravity boosts to help them travel through the solar system. To get a boost, a probe passes by a planet and becomes attracted by its gravity. It is then pulled along by the planet on its orbit around the sun. Some of the planet's orbital speed is transferred to the probe, which is then catapulted towards the next planet to be visited. This slingshot effect is vital, as robot spacecraft could not carry enough fuel to change course from planet to planet. You can see how the slingshot effect works by trying this simple project using a magnet and a steel ball. The second project shows why many of the radio antennae used on the ground and on spacecraft are dish-shaped. The bowl shape of the antenna enables it to collect waves of radio energy. Its curve reflects the waves and brings them together at one point, concentrating all of the collected radio energy.

Slingshot around Jupiter
The space probe *Voyager 2* used several gravity assists to travel around the solar system. To get to Saturn, the probe received a gravity boost from Jupiter. The shells around Jupiter in this artist's visualization represent the gas giant's gravitational field. When *Voyager 2* reached Saturn, it used the slingshot effect again to re-direct itself towards Uranus.

GRAVITY BOOST

You will need: 2 thick books (of equal thickness), 24 x 12-inch piece of thick cardboard, marble-sized steel ball, magnet, 12-inch wooden dowels (x2), tape.

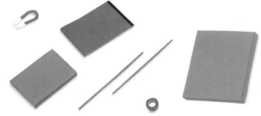

1 Place the books flat on a table 6 inches apart. Lay the piece of cardboard on top of the book, then roll the steel-ball space probe across it. It moves smoothly across the surface.

2 Place the magnet under the cardboard. Roll the steel-ball probe across the card. It is drawn towards the magnet planet by the gravity-like pull of its magnetic field.

3 Tape the magnet to the dowels. Roll the ball and then pull the magnet away. The ball speeds up and is pulled along by the magnet planet, like a probe getting a gravity boost.

MAKE A DISH ANTENNA

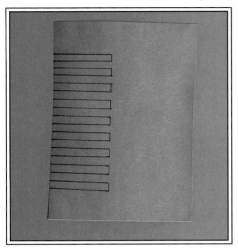

1 Draw 9 thin slits on the postcard using the pencil and ruler. Each slit should measure 1 x ¹/₅ inches. They should be spaced from each other ¹/₅ of an inch apart.

2 Using the scissors, carefully cut out the slits in the postcard. The slits in the card will filter light, splitting it up into thin rays that will reflect off the curve of the antenna.

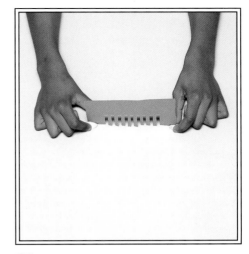

3 Place the large piece of thick cardboard on a table. Stand the postcard 16 inches from one end of the card, with the slits facing down. Fix it in position with modeling clay.

You will need:
plain postcard,
pencil, ruler, scissors,
23¹/₂ x 39-inch piece
of thick cardboard,
modeling clay,
8 x 20-inch strip
of metallic board,
flashlight.

Beaming waves
Dish antennae reflect their collected radio energy onto the receiver. Space probes use their antennae to receive radio signals from mission control on Earth. The receiver can also act as a transmitter, enabling the probe to send back its findings to Earth.

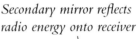

Secondary mirror reflects radio energy onto receiver

Reflector dish

Radio energy

Pivot allows dish to tilt

Receiver

Revolving base

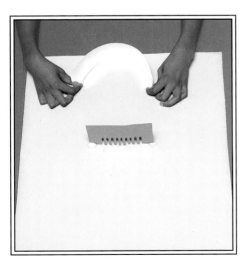

4 Bend the reflective metallic board to form a semi-circular antenna, as shown. Stand it at one end of the thick cardboard base. Then fix it firmly in position using modeling clay.

5 Switch on the flashlight. Direct the light beam so that it shines through the slits in the postcard. The light is split into thin rays, which reflect off the metallic board.

6 Darken the room. Move the flashlight until the light rays reflecting off the curved mirror are brought together at one spot, like radio waves on a dish antenna.

SPACE COMMUNICATIONS

Everyone's lives are affected by modern space technology. Communications satellites (comsats) relay telephone calls around the world and beam television programs directly into our homes. Meteorological satellites provide highly accurate weather forecasts, and navigation satellites tell crews of ships and aircraft exactly where they are. Earth resources satellites study the Earth's oceans, forests and rocks and radio their findings down from space. Collecting information at a distance like this is called remote sensing. Astronomers know infinitely more about the solar system because of information sent back from probes. They also use space technology to look for radio signals produced by intelligent beings elsewhere in the universe.

Comsat

A communications satellite needs antennae to receive and retransmit radio signals. It also needs electricity to power its radio equipment. The comsat's solar cells convert sunlight directly into electricity.

Solar cells

Telstar

On July 10, 1962, the Telstar comsat was launched. It was able to receive messages from the ground, amplify them, and then immediately retransmit them. This made it possible to beam live television broadcasts across the Atlantic Ocean for the first time.

Radio antenna

Omni-directional (all-direction) antenna

Satellite navigation

A geologist checks his position using a hand-held Global Positioning System (GPS) receiver. The GPS is a network of 21 satellites in orbit around the Earth. Radio signals are sent out by the satellites, marking their position in orbit. The receiver picks up signals from at least three of the satellites. This enables the user to pinpoint the receiver's position to within 330 feet.

FACT BOX

• Radio signals sent from Earth to a satellite are called the uplink. Signals sent from a satellite to Earth are called the downlink.

• The first comsat, *Echo 1*, was launched in 1960. The inflatable 108-foot wide comsat resembled a balloon. It was used to reflect radio signals.

ERS-1

The European Earth Resources Satellite (ERS-1) was launched in July, 1991. ERS-1 is an all-weather satellite that can obtain radar images of the Earth's surface at any time of day. It also collects data about phenomena such as winds, waves and ice in the seas and oceans.

Communications dishes

Radio signals are sent to and received from satellites by using large dish antennae. The size of the dish enables it to collect as much energy as possible from the low-power transmitters used by most satellites. Some satellites move across the sky, so the dish has to be able to tilt and turn to follow them.

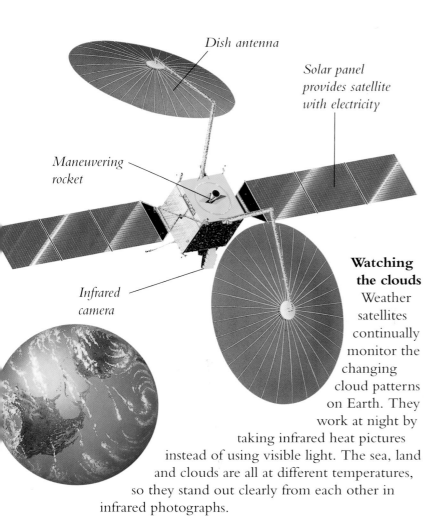

Dish antenna

Solar panel provides satellite with electricity

Maneuvering rocket

Infrared camera

Watching the clouds

Weather satellites continually monitor the changing cloud patterns on Earth. They work at night by taking infrared heat pictures instead of using visible light. The sea, land and clouds are all at different temperatures, so they stand out clearly from each other in infrared photographs.

Monitoring the Earth

This picture of northeastern America was taken by a remote sensing satellite. The images produced by these satellites help to make maps, monitor pollution and study the geology of an area. They are also used to monitor rainforest destruction.

RELAYING RADIO WAVES

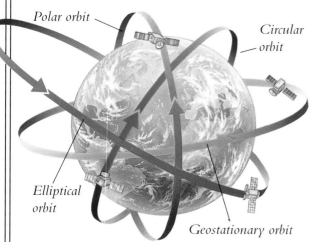

Polar orbit

Circular orbit

Elliptical orbit

Geostationary orbit

Types of orbits
Comsats and weather satellites are usually placed in geostationary orbits. This means that they always face the same part of the Earth. Polar orbits are often chosen for remote-sensing or scientific-survey satellites. As the satellite orbits from pole to pole, the Earth turns below it. In time, the satellite passes over every point on the Earth's surface.

A SATELLITE moves around the Earth in either a circular orbit or an elliptical orbit. It can be positioned in a polar orbit, circling the Earth from pole to pole, or placed in an equatorial orbit around the equator. The satellite may cross the sky several times a day in a low Earth orbit (LEO), or hang in one place, in geostationary orbit. The type of orbit is chosen according to the satellite's function. Most communications and weather satellites are placed in geostationary orbit, about 22,300 miles above the equator. A satellite in this orbit keeps pace with the rotating Earth and appears to hang motionless over the same spot on the ground. Once a radio dish on the ground is aimed at it, the dish does not need to be moved again. Other satellites have to be tracked using movable radio dishes that follow the satellite as it crosses the sky. Try these two simple projects to see for yourself how geostationary orbits work and how satellites relay signals from one place to another.

GEOSTATIONARY ORBIT

You will need: blue card stock, red card stock, scissors, rope, a friend.

1 Cut out 14 strips of blue card stock and 30 strips of red card stock. Use the strips to make a blue circle with a larger red circle around it on the ground. Hold one end of the rope and ask a friend to hold the other end.

2 Walk around the inner circle, while your friend walks around the outer circle. The blue inner circle represents the Earth, and the red outer circle represents the orbit of a satellite around the Earth. If your orbiting friend keeps pace with you as you walk, your human satellite is in a geostationary orbit.

MAKE A SATELLITE RELAY

1 Using the scissors, cut out a rectangle of blue paper just big enough to cover the tin can. Tape it in place. The tin can will act as a ground–based radio receiver.

You will need: blue paper, scissors, tin can, tape, yardstick, thin card stock, flat mirror, modeling clay, flashlight.

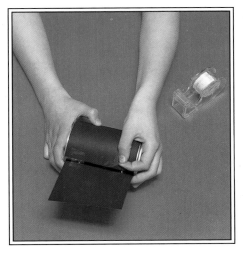

2 Measure out a 4 inch x 4 inch piece of card stock with the ruler. Cut it out and stick it to one side of the tin can. This will act as an antenna on your tin-can receiver.

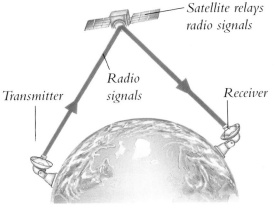

Satellite relays radio signals

Radio signals

Transmitter *Receiver*

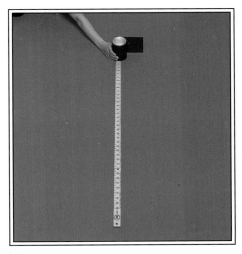

3 Place the tin can on the floor. Take the yardstick and lay it on the floor directly in front of the tin can. Place it on the opposite side to the antenna, as shown.

Redirecting radio waves
Comsats in geostationary orbit above the equator enable radio transmissions to be sent to anywhere on the Earth's surface. Radio signals are transmitted from one side of the planet and aimed at the orbiting satellite. The comsat then relays (redirects) the signal to a receiver on the opposite side of the Earth.

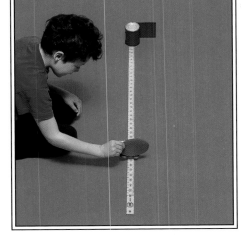

4 Place the mirror on the yardstick about 30 inches from the tin can. The mirror will act like a satellite in geostationary orbit relaying signals. Fix it in place with modeling clay.

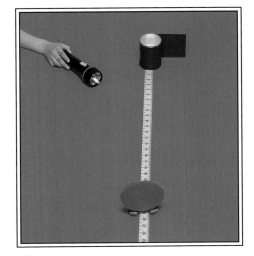

5 Darken the room. Place the flashlight beside the can. The flashlight will send out light beams in the same way that a ground-based transmitter sends out radio waves.

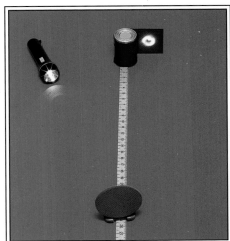

6 Switch on the flashlight. Move the mirror along the ruler. Keep moving it until the light beams are reflected off the mirror satellite and onto the antenna of the tin can.

SPACE PLANES

Integrated aerospike engines

Tail fin

Payload bay

Stub wing

Metallic thermal protection tiles

THE United States space shuttle has proved that crewed spacecraft can be used again and again to ferry people and materials between the Earth's surface and space. As space travel becomes more commonplace, more space planes will be needed, especially when the International Space Station is completed. A fleet of new space planes are being designed and developed around the world. Some of them will be launched with the help of extra rockets or a booster vehicle. Others will be more advanced single-stage-to-orbit (SSTO) craft that will take off under their own power and fly directly into space. Some will be controlled automatically while others will be flown by pilots. American designers are working on the X-33/VentureStar and a hypersonic space plane called Hyper-X. In Germany, a two-stage rocket-plane called Sänger is taking shape. British designers have also developed a plan for a space plane, which they have named Skylon. Several Japanese companies are developing designs for a range of advanced spacecraft including a space plane and an orbiting hotel.

The future
This is an artist's impression of the U.S. VentureStar, a crewed, reusable future space plane. It will be a larger, more advanced version of an automated test vehicle called the X-33. The X-33 measures 65 1/2 in length and 65 1/2 feet across and weighs 124 tons. Results from X-33 test flights will be used in the development of the crewed, full-scale VentureStar spacecraft.

FACT BOX

• VentureStar will be capable of carrying 23 tons of cargo to a height of 115 miles.

• The first rocket plane was designed by Dr. Eugen Sänger and Dr. Irene Bredt in Germany in the 1940s. The 100-ton craft was never built.

• Early space plane designs that were not built include the British MUSTARD and the U.S. Triamese, Bell Bomi and Dyna-Soar.

Launching satellites
VentureStar will perform similar tasks to the Space Shuttle, such as releasing satellites. It is designed to launch vertically using seven built-in aerospike rocket engines. The craft will return to Earth like a glider, using its fins to steer and its fuselage to create lift.

Hypersonic space plane

The experimental X-30 space plane stands in a hangar in this artist's visualization. The X-30 project studied the problems of flying at 25 times the speed of sound. It was cancelled in the mid-1990s, but the lessons learned from it are being used in a new project called Hyper-X.

Testing by computer

Computers are used to test the shape and performance of new aircraft and spacecraft. This avoids the expensive necessity of building scale models and prototypes at every stage. The computer simulation shown here uses false colors to show the stresses of flight on the Sänger space plane's fuselage.

Skylon

This is a model of a possible future spacecraft called Skylon. The Skylon project is a British concept for a pilotless, automated space plane. The vehicle is designed to take off and land horizontally, like a conventional airliner. Skylon's flight into orbit would then be controlled by an advanced neural-net computer. Its versatile wing-tip motors would operate as jet engines in the Earth's atmosphere and as rocket engines in space. The spacecraft's design would enable it to carry a 12-ton payload into orbit.

Sänger separation

The proposed Sänger space plane is designed to separate from its launch vehicle high above the Earth. The rocket-powered launch vehicle would then return to Earth to be prepared for its next flight. The launch vehicle could itself be developed into an airliner capable of flying at more than four times the speed of sound.

FUTURE PROJECTS

REDICTING the future of space exploration is very difficult. It is likely that astronauts will walk on the moon again, and that it will be possible to take holidays in space. It is far less likely that we will travel to the nearest stars in the forseeable future. No one knows exactly when, or if, these events will occur. Exploratory missions are planned to retrieve material from asteroids and to land on comets. This may eventually lead to asteroids being mined. Unmanned probes sent to survey Mars will send back further information to Earth about the planet, which could lead to the human exploration of Mars. Astronauts may return to the moon in the near future to extract valuable minerals from its rocks and bring them back to Earth. Further in the future, a moonbase might serve as a staging post for human exploration of other planets in the solar system.

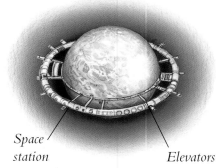

Space station

Elevators

Space elevators
Space projects that seem impossible now may become reality in the very distant future. One day it may be possible to build a giant space station in geostationary orbit all the way around a planet. It could then be connected to the surface of the planet by spoke-like elevators.

International Space Station
This is an artist's impression of how the new International Space Station (ISS) will look when it is completed. The ISS is currently being constructed in orbit around the Earth. It is being built mostly by the United States, with additional modules from Russia, Europe and Japan. The first ISS module was launched from Baikonur, Russia in November 1998.

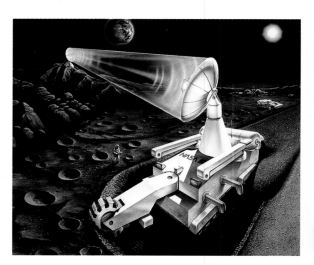

Living on the moon
A moonbase could be built from pre-designed parts, such as the space station modules shown here. The first crews might spend six-month periods on the moon. They would then build larger structures where people would eventually live for years at a time.

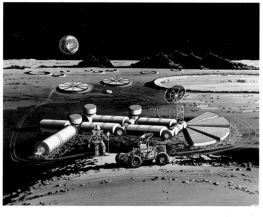

Moon mining
The moon is rich in valuable materials that may one day be extracted by mining. In this artist's visualization, a solar-powered mining machine extract materials from the moon's surface. Lunar soil contains large amounts of oxygen, silicon, iron, titanium and aluminum.

Mission to Mars

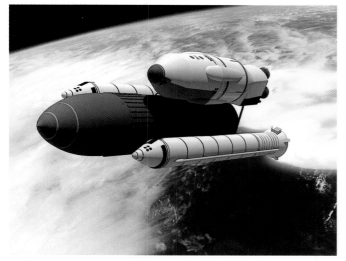

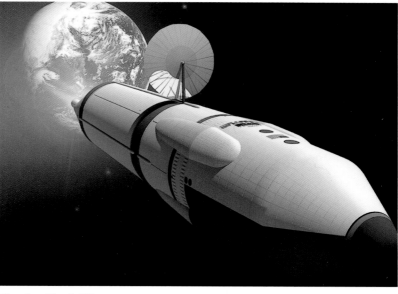

Orbital assembly

If the human exploration of Mars becomes a reality, it could begin with parts of a spacecraft being launched into orbit around the Earth. One proposed vehicle is the U.S. *Mars Explorer 1*. Its components would be carried into space by the space shuttle, or by heavy lift rockets developed from shuttle components. The vehicle would be assembled and tested in orbit.

To the Red Planet

Mars Explorer 1's journey would take between four and nine months, depending on the flight path chosen. With the main spacecraft safely in orbit around Mars, the Lander craft would separate to enter the atmosphere and land on the Martian surface.

Surface transport

Mars mission astronauts might use roving vehicles to explore the Martian surface. Vehicles such as these would enable the astronauts to cover more ground on land surveys and on missions to pick up rock samples.

Shelter and fuel

Astronauts might live on Mars in a shelter sent ahead of the mission. This artist's visualization (*above*) shows a completed Mars outpost in the background, about a mile away from the Lander craft. Fuel for the return journey to Earth might also be sent ahead, or else the astronauts could make it themselves on Mars. In the foreground, a propellant production facility has been set up next to the Lander. Methane and oxygen could be extracted from the atmosphere and used to fuel *Mars Explorer 1* for the return journey.

Index

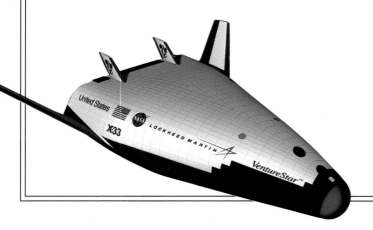